Pies That Inspire

PIES
That Inspire

50 RECIPES FOR CREATIVE AND MODERN FLAVOR COMBINATIONS

Saura Kline

Photography by Darren Muir

ROCKRIDGE PRESS

Interior and Cover Designer: Julie Schrader
Art Producer: Tom Hood
Editors: Reina Glenn and Marjorie DeWitt
Production Editor: Mia Moran
Photography © 2020 Darren Muir. Food styling by Yolanda Muir

ISBN: Print 978-1-64739-993-1 | eBook 978-1-64739-575-9
R0

I dedicate this book to my mom, Martha. You are my best friend, confidant, and number one cheerleader.

Contents

Introduction

There are two types of people in this world: those who don't order dessert, and those who can't *not* order dessert. This book is for the latter. If you're like me, you live, eat, breathe, sleep, and dream about dessert.

Pie is the quintessential American dessert. Pie is about being with friends and family and enjoying each other. Pie is food that brings people together for a celebration, and pie is what this book is all about. "If you love pie so much, why don't you write a book about it?", you may ask. Well, I have, and this is book number two.

I'm a pastry chef, and I've spent a third of my life in professional kitchens making sweet dishes to perfectly complement a delicious meal. I couldn't dream of a better job. And I can't think of a better or more versatile dessert than the all-American pie. It's got everything: layers, crunch, crispy flakes, and creamy fillings. You can make any dessert into a delectable pie, and that is exactly what I've done with many pies in this book. I've been making desserts for people for a long time; I know what works and what doesn't, how to push the limit on creativity without going too far. I like to mix savory and sweet. I like to contrast flavors as well as textures. I've honed my baking style to be out of the box yet nostalgic at times, experimental yet approachable. That's my style, and that's what you'll see in this book.

Food trends come and go, and in my opinion, the humble pie is making a comeback. Gone are the days of standard strawberry-rhubarb and blueberry. We want new, interesting, and surprising ideas. We all have our tried-and-true cherry pie recipe; let's try something else. Let's put a twist on that old classic. Let's transform our favorite cocktail into a mouthwatering pie. Let's see how to pair flavors differently. I couldn't be more excited to share with you my favorite flavor combinations I've dreamed up, transcribed on these pages in pie form. I hope you enjoy them as much as I enjoyed creating them.

CHAPTER 1

There's a New Pie in Town

Pie has been around for centuries. It was first primarily a savory dish—sweet pies weren't common until sugar became affordable in the 16th century. People have been improving upon pies ever since then, modernizing them and introducing new flavors and techniques. In this chapter, I'll go over what you need to know before making a modern pie. From ingredients to equipment, from necessary items to not-so-necessary items, I'll cover it all. These are the tools you'll need to start baking up your modern pie.

PIE, VERSION 2.0

What is pie? Well, it's a crust, a filling, and sometimes a topping. In my previous book, *Easy as Pie*, I went over various traditional methods of how to construct a pie. There is nothing wrong with a classic pie by any means; my favorite pie of all time will forever be a simple peach pie. But there is also nothing wrong with a little creative experimentation.

What can pie become? This book will offer new ideas on how a pie can be improved. It's no longer just plain crust, filling, and topping, friends; I'm introducing you to a whole new world of pie baking. One with flavored crust to enhance the filling. One with layers of fillings complementing each other. And one with more topping possibilities than just whipped cream or meringue. Prepare yourself, because I'll be blurring the boundaries of sweet and savory to thrill your taste buds in new ways. This is pie, version 2.0.

TOOLS OF THE PIE-MAKING TRADE

Before we get started, I want to go over the tools that you'll need before you start your modern pie journey.

Must-Haves

These are the essentials you'll want to have on hand to make a perfect pie.

SCALE

First and foremost, you'll need a trusty kitchen scale. If you want to make recipes consistently and accurately, a kitchen scale is necessary. One cup of flour can weigh a different amount each time you scoop it, and measuring out by volume is actually more work than using a scale for weight. These recipes will list both cup and weight measurements (where applicable), but I encourage you to use a kitchen scale to measure your ingredients, especially for making piecrust. If you've had problems with dough being too dry or too wet before, it's likely you've been using the wrong amount of ingredients. This is why measuring by weight is so important. A decent kitchen scale will only set you back about $10 to $15 and can easily be found at online retailers like Amazon, Walmart, or Webstaurant.

FOOD PROCESSOR

If there is one tool that will save you tons of time, it's this one. The food processor is the answer to all your piecrust needs. It is the easiest tool out there to whip up piecrust in minutes. Don't get me wrong, using a food processor is not the only way to make piecrust, but why not take advantage of our modern equipment if it will save you stress and time? A food processor is a great investment for any home kitchen, and you can easily find a decent one for $50 to $100. All of the crusts in this book are made by food processor simply for the convenience factor.

ROLLING PIN

Rolling pins are more or less a personal preference. If you like a handled one, use that! If you like the tapered ones, by all means. There is no rolling pin out there that will make your pie look and taste any different. Personally, I like to use a smaller rolling pin with handles. I have troubled wrists, and I find that the tapered ones can bother mine more. If you don't have a rolling pin, don't worry. Any cylindrical object will do the trick: a can of nonstick baking spray, a vase, or even a wine bottle. Just be sure the surface of your makeshift rolling pin is nonporous and clean.

PIE PLATES, DISHES, AND PANS

There are many pie plates out there, but I prefer glass dishes overall. I find that they're a great heat conductor for the crust, and it's helpful to see how my crust is cooking. For the recipes in this book, I use a standard shallow 9-inch pie plate, a 9-inch deep-dish pie plate, and sometimes a 9-inch springform pan. I find that certain pies do better in a certain style of dish; however, both a 9-inch shallow pie plate and a 9-inch deep-dish pie plate will work for any of the recipes in this book. Ceramic dishes would be my next favorite, as they also conduct heat well. I like to use those when I'm bringing a pie to a fancy gathering, like Thanksgiving. Aluminum pie plates are convenient alternatives and are usually disposable. But be aware that they are usually smaller than the standard pie plates, and you will likely have to reduce the amount of your filling to fit. When making slab pies, I use the standard 15-by-18-inch jelly roll sheet pan that is easily found in most grocery stores.

Nice-to-Haves

These nonessential tools increase convenience or help you embellish your pie.

Mandoline: A mandoline is an inexpensive tool that allows you to cut paper-thin slices of fruits, vegetables, or anything you might want to slice.

Baking steel: This tool is a little more expensive. Placing your pie on this steel while baking will conduct more heat to the bottom of your crust, which will help prevent the dreaded soggy bottom.

Blender: A blender is a great tool to use in a modern kitchen. Not only can it blend up everyday smoothies, but it can aid in combining new flavors for a modern pie such as blackberry-lemonade puree or corn custard. Sometimes you can find a machine that has both a blender attachment and a food processor.

Pie shield: If you know your oven runs hot, this tool will be a big help. A shield protects the edges of your pie, which usually get darkest first during a bake. Pie shields are very inexpensive, usually under $10.

Cookie cutters: These are a cheap and easy way to embellish your pie. I personally love to use leaves when decorating my pies, but other popular cookie cutter shapes include flowers, hearts, and geometric shapes.

Pastry wheel: This tool makes cutting decorative strips for a pie lattice very easy. Try to find one that combines both a straight edge and a fluted edge in one.

Blowtorch: A blowtorch comes in handy in various ways in a pastry kitchen. It can be used to toast a meringue or to caramelize sugar, also known as brûlée. It is an inexpensive tool easily found online or in baking supply stores.

A PIE-MAKER'S MODERN PANTRY

These are the key ingredients you'll want to keep in stock in your pantry.

Must-Haves

These are absolutely necessary in creating a piecrust. Each crust contains flour, salt, sweetener, fat, and ice water. This is a comprehensive list of exactly what I use and why.

FLOUR

Each pie begins with a crust. And each crust must have a base, which is usually flour. There are many types of flour out there. For most of the recipes in this book, all-purpose flour is the way to go. It's the standard grade of flour that can be used for pastry, bread, pies, and various other applications. I also like to incorporate whole wheat flour because it gives a nutty flavor. Gluten-free flour has no wheat in it and is commonly made up of a combination of rice, sorghum, and other non-gluten flours. I recommend using a gluten-free mix that includes xanthan gum to help with binding, such as Bob's Red Mill 1-to-1 Baking Flour or King Arthur Flour Measure for Measure Flour. Always check ingredient packaging for gluten-free labeling to ensure that the contents were processed in a completely gluten-free facility.

SALT

A little bit of salt goes a long way in baking. If you want your pie to stand out, you'll want to make sure there is just enough salt in your recipe. Just enough can enhance flavor, but too much salt and you can easily ruin a dish. I prefer to use kosher salt in all my baking. I find that the salinity is mild and doesn't vary. I like to use large flaky sea salt, such as Maldon or fleur de sel, as a finishing salt, but not in the dough or filling.

SWEETENER

For the most part, good old granulated sugar is the way to go. It's the most accessible and does the trick. In some recipes, you will need to use brown sugar, corn syrup, or honey instead. Each one provides a unique flavor. If you're feeling ambitious, you can try substituting some of the new sugars out there, such as date sugar, coconut sugar, or agave syrup. These are a popular trend in the baking world and often lend a new level of depth in building flavors.

FAT

There are many fats out there to consider when making piecrust, and I am an all-butter piecrust type of person, through and through. Not only does butter have the best flavor, but I find that it's the easiest to work with and has by far the best mouthfeel and texture. There are other fats out there you can use, such as shortening and lard. Animal fats like duck fat, chicken fat, and bacon fat have also become popular trends. They lend a savory element to the crust and provide more of a crumbly texture. The most important factor is that whatever fat you are using must stay cold to ensure a flaky crust.

ICE WATER

This is one ingredient I know all of us have. It may seem silly to even mention it, but it's important. If you want a flaky piecrust, ice water is a must. Ice water will aid in keeping the fat cold while you're mixing your dough. An ideal pie dough will have tiny little chunks of butter throughout, which will separate layers of flour when baked for the much-desired flaky crust. When preparing your dough, simply fill a cup with some water and drop a couple ice cubes in there; it will make all the difference in the finished product.

Nice-to-Haves

These ingredients are useful additions to your pantry that will help you create the most flavorful fillings and best textures in a pie.

Cocoa powder: An easy way to add a chocolate note to your pie is cocoa powder. A tablespoon is enough to transform your pie into a chocolate lover's dream without having to change anything else in the recipe. It can be used anywhere from the crust to the filling, or even in a whipped or meringue topping. As long as the recipe already has sugar in it, cocoa powder will blend in easily.

Tea leaves: Try using loose tea leaves to impart a unique flavor to your pie. Chamomile, Earl Grey, and green tea are all excellent choices. I particularly like to use them in custards, and they pair great with fruit flavors.

Gelatin: Gelatin is a great way to stabilize custards such as curds or mousses, ensuring a clean-cut slice when finished. It is easily found in the baking aisle at any grocery store. Just make sure you buy the unflavored version.

Cornstarch: Cornstarch is a thickener typically used in fruit pies. A fruit pie baked with cornstarch and one baked without will taste exactly the same; however, one will hold a clean slice and one will not. Though cornstarch is important to the structure of many sweet pies, I recommend forgoing cornstarch in savory pies as it tends to make the filling gummy.

Spirits: Spirits like whiskey, rum, and mezcal can add a really nice touch to any pie filling or topping (the flavor will not come through if added to a crust). I like to give caramel-flavored pies a boozy twist by adding a splash of whiskey or rum, as you'll see in some of the recipes in this book. Mezcal is another great option to use when you want to add a smoky flavor.

Your New Pie Glossary

Blind-baking: Blind-baking is a very common technique used to either partially bake or fully bake a piecrust before it's filled. It is primarily used when making custard pies like quiches or cream pies.

Hand pies: Hand pies are mini pies that can be circular, rectangular, square, or half-moon-shaped. They are composed of two pieces of dough baked with filling inside.

Lattice crust: A lattice crust is a popular design of weaving strips of pie dough together to form a top crust.

Scalloped edge: Also known as a "fluted edge," this term refers to the popular crimping method of pinching a continuous pattern of small semi-circular segments in the crust.

Set up: This term refers to the chill time a custard pie needs in order to firm to the proper consistency. If a custard is not fully set before serving, the pie won't maintain its shape when sliced.

Trim: When dough is rolled out onto a pie plate, there is usually a little extra dough hanging over the pie plate. To trim, use a knife or kitchen scissors to cut off that extra dough.

Vent: When making a pie with a double crust, you always need to vent your pie by cutting little slits into the top crust so that air can escape during the bake. This is also important for hand pies.

THE BASICS OF PIE DOUGH

The crust is the backbone of the pie, and handling the dough correctly can often make or break the finished product. Before you begin experimenting with unconventional pie techniques, make sure you know the basics.

Rolling the Dough

After you've made your dough, you'll follow this process for nearly every pie in this book.

1. Lightly flour your work surface and rolling pin. You may use the same work surface as you did to make your crust, as long as the surface is clean and dry again. Remove one disk of dough from the refrigerator and unwrap the plastic.

2. Use your rolling pin to roll from the center of the dough outward. Turn the dough 90 degrees and roll again from the center out. Continue to roll and turn to get the dough rolled evenly. For a standard 9-inch pie plate, continue to roll out to roughly a 16-inch diameter circle. For a slab pie, you'll want to roll out the dough in a rectangular shape, roughly 16 by 19 inches. For a galette, roll it into a circle with about a 16-inch diameter. If cracks appear in the center or pieces tear off, just patch it back together.

3. When the dough reaches the correct size and shape, transfer it to the baking dish or pan. Starting from one edge of the dough, roll it up onto your rolling pin, as if you were rolling a piece of paper.

4. Lightly spray the pie plate with nonstick baking spray. Unroll your dough onto the pie plate. Press the dough around the sides and into every crevice of your dish to cover it completely.

5. Crimp the edges if it's a single-crust pie. If you'll be adding a top crust, let the edges hang off the sides. Use kitchen shears to trim the dough so that a ½-inch to 1-inch border hangs off the dish (pictured right). For a slab pie, use the same method of rolling up the dough onto your rolling pin, then transfer to a 10-by-15-inch jelly roll pan that has been lightly sprayed with nonstick baking spray. Trim off the edges right to the sides of the pan. It is not necessary to crimp the edges for a slab pie. For a galette, roll your dough onto your rolling pin, then transfer to a sheet pan lined with parchment paper. Since a galette has a more rustic feel to it, you have a lot of room for error. No matter how hard you try, it is tough to ruin a galette, which is excellent news for all.

Blind-Baking

When is it necessary to blind-bake? Well, the answer is not so cut and dried. I only blind-bake crusts for no-bake pies and specific custards that take less time to cook than the crust itself. These include pies such as lemon meringue, banana cream, and most quiches. Since these fillings need less than 20 minutes in the oven, or even no time at all, you'll need to bake your crust before filling it, also known as blind-baking.

Blind-baking is very simple. You'll roll out your dough as usual, transfer it to your pie plate, style the crust as desired, and chill the result thoroughly. Next, you'll cover the dough in the pie plate with parchment paper, and let the edges hang over. If one piece isn't wide enough, turn the plate 90 degrees, pull another piece of parchment paper over the middle, and let the edges hang off the sides. In the center of the piecrust, pour in pie weights, dry beans, or rice. Spread the weights over the entire bottom of the dish. If you find that the parchment paper sticks to the surface of the piecrust too much, try using a little nonstick baking spray. Each recipe will give you the specific blind-baking time and temperature, but in general you will bake in an oven preheated to 375°F for 20 minutes, then remove the pie weights and bake for an additional 15 minutes. Cool completely before filling.

What if I want to mix my dough by hand?

Although the recipes in this book instruct you to make your pie dough in a food processor, it can still be easily done by hand. After all, pie has been around for centuries, while a food processor has most certainly not. To begin, you'll start out by cubing and chilling your butter. Prepare some ice water and set it aside until needed. Place the flour, sugar, and salt in a medium bowl, and mix with a fork or a whisk. Add the cold butter to the flour mixture and use a pastry cutter or a fork to start to cut the butter into the flour. Since this is a task that may take longer than a food processor, you'll want to work quickly to keep the dough cold. If your kitchen is warm, you may want to stick the bowl in the freezer every couple of minutes to ensure that the butter stays cold. Add 1 tablespoon of ice water and continue to mix. Continue to add ice water 1 tablespoon at a time until the butter has been evenly distributed and the dough has formed together. Some butter chunks are okay. Transfer the dough to a clean work surface. Gather the dough together, form it into a disk, and wrap with plastic wrap. Chill the dough for 30 minutes before using.

TECHNIQUES TO ENHANCE YOUR PIES

Let's talk about updated decorative techniques to enhance your pie. After all, we do eat with our eyes first. In this section, I'll cover different ways to spruce up your pie to give it a modern flair. Simple techniques like braiding your lattice, garnishing your pie with sliced fruits, or using various piping tips to decorate are easy to do and really give the finished pie some finesse.

Before You Bake

There are a number of ways you can enhance a pie before it goes into the oven.

Embossed rolling pins: This is a wonderful new kitchen toy that has become more readily available. These pins are easily found online and are very inexpensive. Using an embossed rolling pin works best for pies with a top crust or lattice. Roll out your top crust as usual with a regular rolling pin, then roll over the embossed rolling pin to imprint the design onto the dough. From here, you can cut the dough into lattice strips or use the entire circle of dough to top your pie.

Flavor complements: This is a new technique that is used throughout this book. Why have a pie with a single good flavor when you can complement it with another? I like contrasting flavors, like blueberry and corn, and flavors that enhance one another, like chocolate and caramel. These complements are usually different layers in the same pie, and you might try dreaming up some of your own unique combinations after you get the hang of it by baking a few of these recipes.

Crumble elements: Crumble elements can include so many things, such as nuts, oats, streusels, or a combination of the three. It's a great way to add another level of flavor and texture to a fruit or custard pie. This method is used as a topping for pies that don't have a lattice or double crust.

Coarse or flavored sugars: This method may not be new, but it's still a tasty one. I most often use coarse or flavored sugars when I'm making a pie that has a lattice or double crust. Brush the top crust with a little egg wash, then sprinkle with your sugar of choice. In the oven, the sugar bakes into the crust, creating a wonderfully crisp and sweet texture. I like to use date sugar when I'm making a fall pie, or coconut sugar for a spring/summer pie.

Swirl designs: This method works best for custard pies. Before you bake, swirl some fruit jam, caramel, or chocolate sauce into your custard filling. The best way to do this is to fill a piping bag with two tablespoons of jam or sauce. Pipe lines into the filling, then use a toothpick to swirl it around before you bake.

Lattice and Crimping Procedures

There are many ways you can add to the aesthetic of a pie with lattice and crimping. Here are a few simple techniques.

Traditional Lattice: The classic look never goes out of style.

1. Roll dough out into a circle roughly 16 inches in diameter. Using a sharp knife or pizza cutter alongside a ruler or a sharp straight object to guide you, cut 10 (1-inch) strips from the top to the bottom of dough.

2. Loosely layer 5 dough strips horizontally across the top of a filled pie, about 1 inch apart.

3. Pull back 3 alternating dough strips from right to left and lay one strip down vertically across the center of the pie. Replace the horizontal pieces over the center strip.

4. Pull back the other 2 horizontal strips, stopping where the vertical strip is. Lay down another vertical strip and replace the 2 horizontal strips.

5. Pull back the first 3 alternating strips again and lay down another vertical piece. You should have completed the right side of the pie.

6. Now, going from left to right, pull back 2 alternating dough strips and lay down 1 strip vertically. Replace the horizontal pieces over the vertical strip.

7. Pull back the last 3 horizontal strips and lay down the last vertical strip. Replace the horizontal pieces over the vertical strip. Seal and crimp the edges.

Braids: Cut out three thin strips of dough and braid them. I like to place one or two braided lattice pieces over the top of a pie to offset regular lattice strips. Another way to use braided dough is to lay a long braid around the edges of a piecrust, in lieu of crimping.

Cookie cutters: Use whatever shape you like to add embellishments to your pie. You can do this in four different ways. First, you can cut shapes out of leftover pie dough. Sprinkle with cinnamon sugar (or whatever flavor goes best with your filling) and bake at 350°F until golden brown. Once cooled, you can garnish a custard pie with those cookie shapes. Second, use those same cutout pieces to embellish a lattice-decorated pie. I like to put them around the edges before baking and will use a paring knife to cut "veins" into my dough leaves. Third, use a cookie cutter to punch shapes out of a solid top crust before applying the top crust to a pie before baking. Fourth, use a cookie cutter to make shapes out of all the dough for an entire top crust. Layer the cutouts over the filling to completely top the pie.

Thick crimped crust: Everyone loves a dramatic piecrust. Take any leftover dough and bulk up the edges of your piecrust. Then use your fingers to pinch and press a scalloped pattern around the edges (1). I like to indent each scallop about ¾ inch to 1 inch to really get a nice dramatic border around my pie (2). You can use this method with single-crusted pies, lattice-decorated pies, or double-crusted pies. You may need to prepare more dough, however, to complete this effect.

Twists: To make a twist, simply twirl two thin strips of dough around each other. I like to mix a few twisted pieces of dough with regular strips when I'm making a decorative lattice. Note that it is easiest to twist dough when it is cold.

Cutout scene: This technique is quickly becoming a new pie-decorating trend. After rolling out your top crust, carefully carve out a scene with a sharp knife by cutting out bits of dough. You can print out an image to trace and lay it over the crust if you need a guide. This technique is easier to accomplish before applying the crust to your pie.

After You Bake

There are endless ways to garnish your pie after it comes out of the oven. Here are a few of my favorites.

Brûlée: A simple way to enhance a custard pie is to brûlée the top. Simply sprinkle 1 to 2 tablespoons of coarse sugar on top of a chilled custard pie and use a blowtorch to caramelize the sugars.

Piping: An easy and fun way to dress up your pie is to decorate with a piped whipped topping. Personally, I like to use the Saint Honoré piping tip to make ribbons over the top of my pies. There is no skill involved; the tip does all the work for you.

Citrus slices: Cut a citrus fruit into ¼-inch slices from the pith to the core. Twist the slices and lay them along the border of a pie. This technique works best for custard pies.

Candied berries: This technique works best with round berries, such as cranberries and blueberries. Make a simple syrup by microwaving one tablespoon of water and 1 tablespoon of sugar for 30 seconds. Coat fresh berries in the simple syrup, then dust them with granulated sugar. Let them air dry on a sheet pan lined with a roasting rack for 1 hour before garnishing your pie. In the fall, I like to garnish with candied cranberries and a sprig of fresh rosemary.

Stencils: This method works best for custard pies with no whipped or meringue topping. Lay a decorative stencil on top of your baked pie and dust with cocoa powder, confectioners' sugar, or freeze-dried fruit. Remove the stencil to reveal the design.

TROUBLESHOOTING

Q. Why is there a gap between my filling and top crust?
A. The gap occurs because there is not enough starch to keep the filling from deflating during the bake. The heat of the oven causes the filling to expand, and if there is not enough starch in the recipe, then it will just deflate after it has cooled. Add 1 to 2 more tablespoons of cornstarch or flour to your recipe.

Q. Why is my crust turning too dark before my filling is done?
A. Some ovens run hotter than others. A piecrust shield is a popular tool that can be used to prevent a crust from browning too fast. Place the piecrust shield over the pie for the first 20 minutes of the bake. Remove the piecrust shield and continue to bake as directed in the instructions.

Q. How can I prevent a soggy bottom?
A. There are a few ways to prevent soggy bottoms. You can partially blind-bake your crust first, then add the filling and continue to bake the pie per instructions. Or you can use a baking steel to help conduct more heat to the bottom of your pie. Preheat the oven with the steel inside and place the pie on top of the steel when baking.

Q. Why did my custard crack in the oven?
A. There are two possible reasons: It's been baked too long, or the oven temperature is too high. Try turning down the oven by 25 degrees or baking for 5 minutes less.

Q. Why did my fruit pie not slice well?
A. Either you've cut the pie too soon after it finished baking, or there is not enough starch in the recipe. A fruit pie needs to cool for 2 to 4 hours before cutting to allow the starches to set up. But if the pie is fully cooled and still won't set up, try adding 2 more tablespoons of starch to the recipe before you bake it the next time.

ABOUT THE RECIPES

These aren't your typical pie recipes. When my mind wanders at night, I dream up new flavors to put together. Sometimes they work in real life and sometimes they don't, but I'm always inventing and experimenting. I love mixing flavors together in layers and using out-of-the-box toppings to enhance my pies. When coming up with the recipes in this book, I tried to implement accessible ingredients anyone can find in a standard grocery store and use them in new and innovative ways that anyone can replicate. These pies are unique, yet approachable. They are modern interpretations of my favorite flavor combinations, and I hope you love them as much as I do.

Each recipe includes a list of the equipment you'll need, the total time required to make the pie, and both weight and volume measurements (where applicable) for your convenience.

CHAPTER 2

The New Crusts

Ah, piecrust, wonderful vessel of tender flaky delight, how we love thee. The basis of every pie starts with piecrust, and this chapter covers all types of it, from my all-butter piecrust to a sweet cocoa crust, a savory whole wheat, and a nutty cornmeal. There's even a gluten-free version that you can use in place of any piecrust in this book.

ALL-BUTTER CRUST

Yield: Single crust for a 9-inch standard pie or deep-dish pie
Total time: 40 minutes

Look no further for the ultimate piecrust. This all-butter recipe is my tried and true, and the most universal. It can be used with sweet or savory fillings, for hand pies or slab pies, for single or double crusts. This crust easily fits in a standard or deep-dish pie tin, and when doubled yields just a little extra to use for design pieces. It's my favorite to use for most pies; the texture is just the right amount of flaky and tender you want in a piecrust.

Equipment: Knife, metal bowl, food processor, measuring cups or kitchen scale, measuring spoons, plastic wrap

---

8 tablespoons cold unsalted butter (113 grams)

1¼ cups all-purpose flour (160 grams)

1½ teaspoons granulated sugar

¼ teaspoon salt

2 to 3 tablespoons ice water

1. Cut the butter into small cubes, then place them in a metal bowl and put the bowl in the freezer until needed.

2. In a food processor, pulse the flour, sugar, and salt to combine. Add the chilled butter cubes and process for 30 seconds until the mixture looks like dry crumbles. Add 1 tablespoon of ice water and process for 20 seconds. Continue adding ice water, 1 tablespoon at a time and processing for 20 seconds after each addition, until the dough comes together in large chunks. Turn off the machine and transfer the dough to a clean, dry work surface.

3. Gather the dough together and form it into a smooth ball, then press it into a disk. Wrap the disk with plastic wrap.

4. Place the dough in the refrigerator for at least 30 minutes, or up to 3 days. After 30 minutes, the dough will be at the perfect temperature and texture to roll. If you have chilled the dough for longer, you will need to let the dough come to room temperature for approximately 30 minutes before you can roll it out.

GLUTEN-FREE CRUST

Yield: Single crust for a 9-inch standard pie or deep-dish pie
Total time: 40 minutes

Most of us have people in our life who follow a gluten-free diet, and they deserve pie, too. Pie does not discriminate; all are welcome to enjoy. This is an easy pie-crust to make, and if you didn't already know it was gluten-free, you may not even notice. The crust is made by laminating layers together, emulating a traditional piecrust. It can be baked at the same temperatures and same times as the All-Butter Crust, so feel free to use them interchangeably in any recipe.

Equipment: Knife, metal bowl, food processor, measuring cups or kitchen scale, measuring spoons, parchment paper, plastic wrap

---

6 tablespoons cold unsalted butter (85 grams)

1½ cups gluten-free flour (255 grams)

1 tablespoon granulated sugar (13 grams)

½ teaspoon salt

¼ teaspoon baking powder

½ cup sour cream (123 grams)

1 to 2 tablespoons ice water

1. Cut the butter into small cubes, then place them in a metal bowl and put the bowl in the freezer until needed.

2. In a food processor, pulse the flour, sugar, salt, and baking powder a few times to combine.

3. Add the butter and turn the food processer on for 30 seconds. Add the sour cream and process until the dough starts to form into large crumbles. Add the ice water, 1 tablespoon at a time and process-ing for 20 seconds after each addition, until the dough comes together in large chunks. Turn off the machine and transfer the dough to a clean, dry work surface.

4. Form the dough into a ball. In order to achieve a flaky crust, roll the dough into an 8-by-8-inch square between two pieces of parchment paper. Fold one half into the center of the dough, then the other half, like folding a letter. Turn the dough

90 degrees and repeat this step two more times. Form the dough into a round disk and wrap with plastic wrap.

5. Chill the dough in the refrigerator for at least 30 minutes, or up to 3 days. If you have chilled the dough for longer, you will need to let the dough come to room temperature for approximately 30 minutes before you can roll it out. Alternately, freeze the dough for up to 6 months.

WHOLE WHEAT CRUST WITH THYME

Yield: Single crust for a 9-inch standard pie or deep-dish pie
Total time: 40 minutes

Whole wheat flour gives pie dough a sweet, almost nutty flavor that complements nearly any filling. I sneak fresh herbs into dessert whenever I can, and the added thyme here gives the crust a slightly floral herbaceous note.

Equipment: Knife, metal bowl, food processor, measuring cups or kitchen scale, measuring spoons, plastic wrap

---

8 tablespoons cold unsalted butter (113 grams)

¾ cup whole wheat flour (90 grams)

½ cup all-purpose flour (64 grams)

1½ teaspoons granulated sugar

¼ teaspoon salt

1 tablespoon fresh thyme leaves

2 to 3 tablespoons ice water

1. Cut the butter into small cubes, place them in a metal bowl, and leave the bowl in the freezer until needed.

2. In a food processor, pulse the whole wheat flour, all-purpose flour, sugar, salt, and thyme to combine. Add the chilled butter cubes and process for 30 seconds, or until the mixture looks like dry crumbles. Add 1 tablespoon of ice water and process for 20 seconds. Continue adding ice water, 1 tablespoon at a time and processing for 20 seconds after each addition, until the dough comes together in large chunks. Turn off the machine and transfer the dough to a clean, dry work surface.

3. Gather the dough together and form it into a smooth ball, then press it into a disk. Wrap the disk with plastic wrap.

4. Place the dough in the refrigerator for at least 30 minutes, or up to 3 days. After 30 minutes, the dough will be at the perfect temperature and texture to roll. If you have chilled the dough for longer, you will need to let the dough come to room temperature for approximately 30 minutes before you can roll it out.

CORNMEAL CRUST

Yield: Single crust for a 9-inch standard pie or deep-dish pie
Total time: 40 minutes

Cornmeal is a flavor that pairs well with both sweet and savory pies, with a fresh fruit pie or a gooey, cheesy hand pie. I've added just a touch of honey in this recipe to enhance the sweetness of the corn. The finer the cornmeal, the better, but polenta will also work if you can't find cornmeal.

Equipment: Knife, metal bowl, food processor, measuring cups or kitchen scale, measuring spoons, plastic wrap

6 tablespoons cold unsalted butter (85 grams)

1 cup all-purpose flour (145 grams)

½ cup cornmeal (75 grams)

1½ teaspoons granulated sugar

1½ teaspoons honey

¼ teaspoon salt

1 egg

1 to 2 tablespoons ice water

1. Cut the butter into small cubes, place them in a metal bowl, and leave the bowl in the freezer until needed.

2. In a food processor, pulse the flour, cornmeal, sugar, honey, and salt to combine. Add the chilled butter cubes and egg. Process for 30 seconds, or until the mixture looks like dry crumbles. Add 1 tablespoon of ice water and process for 20 seconds. Continue adding ice water, 1 tablespoon at a time and processing for 20 seconds after each addition, until the dough comes together in large chunks. Turn off the machine and transfer the dough to a clean, dry work surface.

3. Gather the dough together and form it into a smooth ball, then press it into a disk. Wrap the disk with plastic wrap.

4. Place the dough in the refrigerator for at least 30 minutes, or up to 3 days. After 30 minutes, the dough will be at the perfect temperature and texture to roll. If you have chilled the dough for longer, you will need to let the dough come to room temperature for approximately 30 minutes before you can roll it out.

COCOA CRUST

Yield: Single crust for a 9-inch standard pie or deep-dish pie
Total time: 40 minutes

Chocolate makes everything better, right? This cocoa crust is the chocolate version of my flaky All-Butter Crust. It's sweet but not too sweet, and it adds just a little more chocolaty richness to pies that already have a little chocolate in them. This crust whips up easily in the food processor and is a simple way to enhance the flavor of your pie.

Equipment: Knife, metal bowl, food processor, measuring cups or kitchen scale, measuring spoons, plastic wrap

8 tablespoons cold unsalted butter (113 grams)

1 cup plus 2 tablespoons all-purpose flour (162 grams)

2 tablespoons cocoa powder (15 grams)

1 tablespoon granulated sugar (13 grams)

¼ teaspoon salt

2 to 3 tablespoons ice water

1. Cut the butter into small cubes, place them in a metal bowl, and leave the bowl in the freezer until needed.

2. In a food processor, pulse the flour, cocoa powder, sugar, and salt to combine. Add the chilled butter cubes and process for 30 seconds, or until the mixture looks like dry crumbles. Add 1 tablespoon of ice water and process for 20 seconds. Continue adding ice water, 1 tablespoon at a time and processing for 20 seconds after each addition, until the dough comes together in large chunks. Turn off the machine and transfer the dough to a clean, dry work surface.

3. Gather the dough together and form it into a smooth ball, then press it into a disk. Wrap the disk with plastic wrap.

4. Place the dough in the refrigerator for at least 30 minutes, or up to 3 days. After 30 minutes, the dough will be at the perfect temperature and texture to roll.

Purple Sweet Potato Pie Brûlée, page 31

CHAPTER 3

New Takes on Old Classics

We all have our favorite classic pies, but how can we improve on these well-known desserts? This chapter showcases modern embellishments on some traditional classics. Whether it's a new flavor combination, an inventive crust, or a creative design, these pies all feature a contemporary twist.

STRAWBERRY CHESS PIE

Yield: 1 (9-inch) standard pie **Total time:** 3 hours 50 minutes

Chess pie is an old-school Southern pie. Some people know it and love it, and some have never heard of it. I think it's a delicious custard pie and wanted to bring it back with a summery twist. All of my favorite flavors come to life in the summer, including corn and strawberry. A sweet vegetable, corn is great in desserts and pairs wonderfully with fruit. To me, this pie tastes like a slice of strawberry corn-bread in pie form. The slices of fresh berries on top give this pie a beautiful finish.

Equipment: Rolling pin, 9-inch pie plate, mixing bowl, whisk, measuring cups or kitchen scale, measuring spoons, knife

---

Single batch Cornmeal Crust (page 25)

1½ cups granulated sugar (300 grams)

¼ cup whole milk (61 grams)

¼ cup strawberry jam (61 grams)

4 eggs

1 tablespoon cornmeal (9 grams)

1 teaspoon vanilla extract

½ teaspoon salt

1 tablespoon apple cider vinegar (14 grams)

5 fresh strawberries to garnish

1. Prepare a batch of the Cornmeal Crust.

2. Preheat the oven to 350°F. Unwrap the dough onto a lightly floured work surface. Lightly flour a rolling pin and begin rolling from the center outward. Roll the dough into a circle roughly 16 inches in diameter. Drape the dough over your rolling pin, then transfer to a pie plate. Trim and crimp the edges. Freeze the piecrust for 10 minutes while preparing the filling.

3. In a medium bowl, whisk together the sugar, whole milk, strawberry jam, eggs, cornmeal, vanilla, and salt. Whisk in the apple cider vinegar. Pour the filling into the chilled crust. Bake for 1 hour, or until the center is set and does not appear liquid. Chill in the refrigerator for at least 2 hours.

4. To garnish, slice fresh strawberries lengthwise and lay them over the top of the chilled pie. Cover the entire surface with fresh strawberries, overlapping the slices slightly if needed. Chill until ready to serve.

PURPLE SWEET POTATO PIE BRÛLÉE

Yield: 1 (9-inch) deep-dish pie **Total time:** 4 hours 35 minutes

I like a flair for the dramatic, and this pie delivers with its vibrant purple color. In this recipe, bright purple potatoes make for a wonderful twist on the classic sweet potato pie. I also brûlée the top of the custard to give this pie a modern update and some great texture for your bite.

Equipment: Fork, baking sheet, rolling pin, 9-inch deep-dish pie plate, food processor, measuring cups or kitchen scale, measuring spoons, blowtorch

Single batch Gluten-Free Crust (page 22), or All-Butter Crust (page 20) if not gluten-free

1¼ pounds purple sweet potatoes (2 to 3 potatoes)

1 (12-ounce) can evaporated milk

¾ cup granulated sugar, divided (150 grams)

3 eggs

3 tablespoons melted unsalted butter (42 grams)

1 teaspoon vanilla extract

½ teaspoon ground cinnamon

½ teaspoon ground ginger

½ teaspoon salt

¼ teaspoon ground nutmeg

1. Prepare a batch of the Gluten-Free Crust or All-Butter Crust.

2. Preheat the oven to 400°F. Prick the sweet potatoes all over several times with a fork and roast on a baking sheet for 1 hour, or until tender. Let the potatoes cool completely.

3. Preheat the oven to 350°F. Unwrap the dough onto a lightly floured work surface. Lightly flour a rolling pin and begin rolling from the center outward. Roll the dough into a circle roughly 16 inches in diameter. Drape the dough over your rolling pin, then transfer to a deep-dish pie plate. Trim and crimp the edges. Freeze the piecrust for 10 minutes.

4. Remove the flesh from the cooled sweet potatoes. In a food processor, combine the sweet potato flesh, evaporated milk, ½ cup of sugar (100 grams), eggs, melted butter, vanilla, cinnamon, ginger, salt, and nutmeg. Puree until smooth. Pour the filling into the chilled crust. Bake for 45 minutes. Chill in the refrigerator for at least 2 hours.

5. To serve, sprinkle the remaining ¼ cup of sugar (50 grams) over the top of the pie. Use a blowtorch to caramelize the sugar.

BLACKBERRY-LEMONADE ICEBOX PIE WITH BROWN BUTTER GRAHAM CRUST

Yield: 1 (9-inch) deep-dish pie **Total time:** 1 hour 20 minutes

Here's the scenario: It's summertime and you want to make a pie, but you don't have much time and definitely don't want to heat up your house for too long. The solution: this twist on a lemonade icebox pie. Blackberries and lemons blend together for an easy filling, the pie only bakes for 6 minutes, and it's all ready to serve in just over an hour. This pie is perfectly tart with just enough sweetness, and the fruit filling is complemented by the nutty notes of the browned-butter graham crust.

Equipment: Saucepan, mixing bowls, measuring cups or kitchen scale, measuring spoons, spatula, 9-inch deep-dish pie plate, blender, whisk

FOR THE BROWNED-BUTTER GRAHAM CRUST

10 tablespoons unsalted butter (141 grams)

2 cups graham cracker crumbs, from 12 sheets of crackers (170 grams)

¼ cup brown sugar (50 grams)

¼ teaspoon salt

Nonstick baking spray

TO MAKE THE BROWNED-BUTTER GRAHAM CRUST

1. In a small saucepan, heat the butter over medium-high heat until the butter has melted fully. Continue to cook the butter until the milk solids caramelize and the butter appears foamy. It will smell nutty. Remove from the heat. In a large bowl, combine the graham cracker crumbs, sugar, and salt, then pour in the butter. Mix with a spatula to combine. Lightly spray a deep-dish pie plate with nonstick baking spray. Pour the graham cracker mixture into the pie plate. Press the crumbs down firmly in the bottom and up the sides to create the crust. Chill the crust in the refrigerator while preparing the filling.

FOR THE BLACKBERRY-LEMONADE FILLING

¾ cup freshly
   squeezed lemon
   juice (172 grams)

½ cup fresh
   blackberries
   (76 grams)

2 (14-ounce)
   cans sweetened
   condensed milk

Grated zest of 1 lemon

¼ cup sour cream
   (57 grams)

TO MAKE THE BLACKBERRY-LEMONADE FILLING

2. Preheat the oven to 350°F. In a blender, combine
    the lemon juice and blackberries and blend them
    well. In a medium bowl, combine the sweetened
    condensed milk, lemon zest, sour cream, and
    blended juice. Whisk until smooth. Pour the filling
    into the chilled crust and bake for 6 minutes. Chill
    in the refrigerator for 1 hour before serving.

Fancy it up: Slice 1 lemon thinly. Garnish the
chilled pie with the lemon slices and more
fresh blackberries.

COCONUT AND KEY LIME PIE WITH CARAMELIZED COCONUT

Yield: 1 (9-inch) deep-dish pie **Total time:** 1 hour 30 minutes

Key lime pie is such a classic favorite. It's made up of a sweet, crumbly base, a tart filling, and a whipped topping. I thought it would be a great idea to combine this popular pie with another favorite: the coconut cream pie. For this mashup, I've made a base of graham cracker crust, a layer of caramelized coconut, a tart key lime filling, and a luscious coconut whipped topping made only with coconut cream. With its perfect layers of contrasting texture and flavor, this pie is heaven in a bite.

Equipment: Food processor, measuring cups or kitchen scale, measuring spoons, 9-inch deep-dish pie plate, saucepan, mixing bowl, zester, whisk, stand mixer with whisk attachment, spatula

FOR THE GRAHAM CRACKER CRUST

2 cups of graham cracker crumbs, from 12 sheets of crackers (170 grams)

¼ cup granulated sugar (50 grams)

¼ teaspoon salt

8 tablespoons melted unsalted butter (113 grams)

Nonstick baking spray

TO MAKE THE GRAHAM CRACKER CRUST

1. Preheat the oven to 350°F. In a food processor, combine the graham cracker crumbs, sugar, and salt. Stream in the melted butter. Pulse until all crumbs are wet. Lightly spray a deep-dish pie plate with nonstick baking spray. Pour the graham cracker mixture into the pie plate. Press the crumbs down firmly in the bottom and up the sides to create the crust. Bake for 10 minutes.

TO MAKE THE CARAMELIZED COCONUT

2. In a small saucepan, combine the shredded coconut, coconut milk, sugar, and salt. Cook over high heat for 10 minutes, or until all the coconut milk has evaporated and the shredded coconut starts to caramelize. When the crust is out of the oven, pour the caramelized coconut over the top. Smooth the coconut into an even layer, then set aside.

FOR THE CARAMELIZED COCONUT

2 cups shredded coconut (200 grams)

½ cup coconut milk (113 grams)

¼ cup granulated sugar (50 grams)

¼ teaspoon salt

FOR THE KEY LIME FILLING

2 (14-ounce) cans sweetened condensed milk

¾ cup freshly squeezed key lime juice (172 grams)

½ cup sour cream (123 grams)

1 tablespoon grated lime zest

FOR THE COCONUT WHIPPED CREAM

2 cans coconut cream, chilled in the refrigerator overnight (454 grams)

½ cup confectioners' sugar (60 grams)

TO MAKE THE KEY LIME FILLING

3. In a medium bowl, combine the sweetened condensed milk, lime juice, sour cream, and lime zest. Whisk until smooth. Pour the filling over the caramelized coconut and bake for 6 minutes. The center should appear set and not liquid. Chill the pie in the refrigerator for 1 hour.

TO MAKE THE COCONUT WHIPPED CREAM

4. Remove the cans from the refrigerator and pour the contents into the bowl of a stand mixer fitted with a whisk attachment. Add the confectioners' sugar and whip on medium-high speed until soft peaks form. Top the chilled pie with the coconut whipped topping and smooth it out with a spatula. Chill in the refrigerator until ready to serve.

Fancy it up: Try using a Saint Honoré piping tip to pipe on your coconut whipped topping. It's an easy way to create beautiful ribbons of topping, and it's easily sourced from Amazon or a local baking supplies store.

RHUBARB AND CHAMOMILE CUSTARD PIE

Yield: 1 (9-inch) standard pie **Total time:** 2 hours 5 minutes

Nothing screams spring to me quite like rhubarb, and I decided to modernize the classic rhubarb pie with some interesting flavors and designs. I love the tart flavor, and pairing it with tea seemed like a no-brainer to me. In this recipe, I combine a chamomile custard pie with a layer of sweet and tangy rhubarb jam. To go even further, I top the jam with a layer of poached rhubarb and weave it into a lattice design. Don't be alarmed; it's actually easier than it sounds.

Equipment: Rolling pin, 9-inch pie plate, parchment paper, pie weights, mixing bowl, measuring cups or kitchen scale, measuring spoons, small saucepan, large pot, peeler, knife

---

FOR THE CRUST

Single batch
   All-Butter Crust
   (page 20)

FOR THE CHAMOMILE CUSTARD

¾ cup granulated
   sugar (150 grams)

¾ cup heavy cream
   (170 grams)

3 eggs

¼ cup flour
   (32 grams)

2½ teaspoons
   chamomile leaves

½ teaspoon
   vanilla extract

¼ teaspoon salt

TO BLIND-BAKE THE CRUST

1. Prepare a batch of the All-Butter Crust.

2. Preheat the oven to 375°F. Unwrap the dough on a lightly floured work surface. Lightly flour a rolling pin and begin rolling from the center outward. Roll the dough into a circle roughly 16 inches in diameter. Drape the dough over your rolling pin, then transfer to a pie plate. Trim and crimp the edges. Freeze the piecrust for 10 minutes.

3. Remove the piecrust from the freezer. Lay a large piece of parchment paper over the center of the dish and fill with pie weights. Blind-bake the crust for 20 minutes.

TO MAKE THE CHAMOMILE CUSTARD

4. In a large bowl, combine the sugar, heavy cream, eggs, flour, chamomile leaves, vanilla, and salt and mix well. Fill the blind-baked piecrust with the custard. Reduce the heat to 325°F and bake for 45 minutes. Cool completely in the refrigerator.

FOR THE RHUBARB JAM

1¼ pounds rhubarb, roughly chopped

½ cup granulated sugar (100 grams)

¼ cup water

2 tablespoons freshly squeezed lemon juice (28 grams)

1 teaspoon vanilla extract

½ teaspoon grated lemon zest

FOR THE RHUBARB LATTICE

2 cups water

1 cup granulated sugar (200 grams)

3 or 4 rhubarb stalks

5. In a small saucepan over medium heat, combine the rhubarb, sugar, water, lemon juice, vanilla, and lemon zest and cook for about 10 minutes, or until the rhubarb has broken down and the sauce appears thick. Spoon the jam over the chilled chamomile custard and return the pie plate to the refrigerator until cooled.

TO MAKE THE RHUBARB LATTICE

6. In a large pot over medium heat, heat the water and sugar to make simple syrup. Peel 3 to 4 stalks of rhubarb to get 14 to 16 thick strips. Poach the strips in the simple syrup for about 45 seconds, or until slightly softened. Lay the strips on a piece of parchment paper to cool.

7. On the chilled pie, lay 7 or 8 strips down vertically, sitting right next to each other, and 7 or 8 strips horizontally, alternating strips over and under in a woven pattern. Use a sharp knife to trim the excess rhubarb strips around the edges of the pie. Chill in the refrigerator until ready to serve.

Don't have that? Earl Grey would be a great substitution if you don't have chamomile tea. Just swap in the same amount of tea leaves.

BLUEBERRY-MINT PIE WITH LEMON-RICOTTA WHIPPED CREAM

Yield: 1 (9-inch) standard pie **Total time:** 2 hours 25 minutes

A classic blueberry pie is hard to beat, but I challenge you to try this variation. Just the right amount of citrus makes the blueberry flavor pop, and a little bit of fresh mint really goes a long way. It brightens up the blueberry flavor even more and is heavenly paired with a lemon-ricotta whipped cream. I recommend a modern braided lattice design for this pie. It consists of 5 strips weaving each way, with 1 strip braided in each direction. Feel free to do a simple lattice instead or even just a top crust if you like.

Equipment: Rolling pin, 9-inch pie plate, mixing bowls, measuring cups or kitchen scale, measuring spoons, zester, whisk, pastry brush, pastry wheel, knife, stand mixer with whisk attachment

---

FOR THE CRUST

Double batch Gluten-Free Crust (page 22), or All-Butter Crust (page 20) if not gluten-free

1 egg

2 tablespoons water

TO MAKE THE CRUST

1. Prepare a double batch of the Gluten-Free Crust or All-Butter Crust.

2. Preheat the oven to 350°F. Unwrap one disk of dough onto a lightly floured work surface. Lightly flour a rolling pin and begin rolling from the center outward. Roll the dough into a circle roughly 16 inches in diameter. Drape the dough over your rolling pin and transfer to a pie plate. Let the edges hang over for now. Freeze the piecrust for 10 minutes.

TO MAKE THE BLUEBERRY FILLING

3. In a large bowl, mix together the blueberries, sugar, cornstarch, lemon juice, lemon zest, and mint. Toss to coat everything, then pour over the chilled piecrust.

FOR THE BLUEBERRY FILLING

2 pounds fresh or frozen blueberries

¾ cup granulated sugar (150 grams)

¼ cup cornstarch (30 grams)

2 tablespoons freshly squeezed lemon juice (28 grams)

Grated zest of 1 lemon

1 tablespoon finely chopped fresh mint

FOR THE LEMON-RICOTTA WHIPPED CREAM

1 cup full-fat ricotta (226 grams)

½ cup heavy cream (113 grams)

¼ cup confectioners' sugar (30 grams)

Grated zest of 1 lemon

TO MAKE THE LATTICE

4. In a small bowl, whisk together the eggs and water to make an egg wash. Use a pastry brush to brush the egg wash over the edges of the pie, then set the remaining egg wash aside. Unwrap the other disk of dough onto a lightly floured work surface. Lightly flour a rolling pin and begin rolling from the center outward. Roll dough into a 12-by-18-inch rectangle. Use a knife or a pastry wheel to cut 6 (¼-inch) strips and 8 (1-inch) strips.

5. Weave 2 (3-strand) braids out of the ¼-inch strips. Arrange 4 of the 1-inch strips and 1 braid over the filled pie from top to bottom. Take every other strip and fold it from the bottom to the top. Lay the other braid down horizontally, then fold the strips back down. Continue this step with the remaining 1-inch strips, alternating strips to fold up each time.

6. Trim the edges to hang ½ inch over the pie plate. Roll up the edges to form a crust around the edge of the pie plate. Brush the remaining egg wash over the entire pie. Freeze for 10 minutes before baking. Bake for 1 hour 30 minutes. Cool at room temperature for at least 2 hours before serving.

TO MAKE THE LEMON-RICOTTA WHIPPED CREAM

7. In a stand mixer fitted with a whisk attachment, whip the ricotta, heavy cream, confectioners' sugar, and lemon zest until stiff peaks form. Serve the pie with the whipped cream on the side.

CORN AND BLUEBERRY PIE WITH CARAMEL CORN AND CORNMEAL CRUST

Yield: 1 (9-inch) deep-dish pie **Total time:** 5 hours 40 minutes

I know, you're probably thinking, "How many times can the word *corn* be in the title of a pie?" Well, let's just go with three. Each type of corn in this recipe imparts a very important layer of flavor. To begin, we start with a Cornmeal Crust. A layer of sweet corn custard is next, followed by a vibrant and fruity blueberry jam. To top it off, I just had to add caramel corn. I hope you'll find that this pie is just as fun to create as it is to eat.

Equipment: Rolling pin, 9-inch deep-dish pie plate, parchment paper, pie weights, mixing bowls, measuring cups or kitchen scale, measuring spoons, food processor, saucepans, blender, fine-mesh strainer, spatula, whisk, sheet pan, parchment paper or aluminum foil

FOR THE CRUST

Single batch Cornmeal Crust (page 25)

FOR THE CORN CUSTARD

2 tablespoons cold water

2 teaspoons gelatin powder

3 cups fresh or frozen corn (525 grams)

2 cups heavy cream (454 grams)

½ cup granulated sugar (100 grams)

1 teaspoon salt

TO BLIND-BAKE THE CRUST

1. Prepare a batch of the Cornmeal Crust.

2. Preheat the oven to 375°F. Unwrap the dough onto a lightly floured work surface. Lightly flour a rolling pin and begin rolling from the center outward. Roll the dough into a circle roughly 16 inches in diameter. Drape the dough over your rolling pin, then transfer to a deep-dish pie plate. Trim and crimp the edges. Freeze the piecrust for 10 minutes.

3. Remove the piecrust from the freezer. Lay a large piece of parchment paper over the center of the dish and fill with pie weights. Blind-bake in the preheated oven for 20 minutes. Remove the weights and bake for an additional 15 minutes. Cool completely at room temperature (about 15 minutes while you make the custard).

continued >

FOR THE BLUEBERRY JAM

2 cups fresh or
  frozen blueberries
  (200 grams)

¼ cup granulated
  sugar (50 grams)

2 tablespoons freshly
  squeezed lemon
  juice (28 grams)

Grated zest of 1 lemon

¼ teaspoon pectin

FOR THE CARAMEL CORN

4 cups plain popcorn

3 tablespoons
  unsalted butter
  (42 grams)

¼ cup brown sugar
  (50 grams)

2 tablespoons
  light corn syrup
  (41 grams)

¼ teaspoon salt

¼ teaspoon
  baking soda

TO MAKE THE CORN CUSTARD

4. In a small bowl, combine the cold water and gelatin powder and set aside to let the gelatin bloom. In a medium saucepan over high heat, combine the corn, heavy cream, sugar, and salt and heat until boiling. Transfer the mixture to a blender and blend until very smooth. Strain through a fine-mesh strainer into a medium bowl and discard the corn skins. Mix the bloomed gelatin into the corn custard and pour it into the piecrust. Chill in the refrigerator for at least 2 hours.

TO MAKE THE BLUEBERRY JAM

5. In a small saucepan, combine the blueberries, sugar, lemon juice, lemon zest, and pectin. Toss to coat everything, then turn the heat on medium-high. Cook for 10 minutes, or until the blueberries have broken down and the mixture appears thick. Pour the jam over the top of the corn custard and use a spatula to smooth it out, creating an even layer of jam. Chill the pie in the refrigerator for at least 2 hours, until ready to serve.

TO MAKE THE CARAMEL CORN

6. Preheat the oven to 275°F. In a large bowl, set aside the popcorn. In a small saucepan over high heat, melt the butter, brown sugar, corn syrup, and salt together. Once melted, boil for 1 to 2 minutes. Remove from the heat and whisk in the baking soda. Quickly pour the mixture over the popcorn and toss to evenly coat. Transfer to a sheet pan lined with parchment paper or aluminum foil. Bake for 10 minutes, stirring halfway through. Cool completely at room temperature before breaking into pieces. Top the pie with the caramel corn only when ready to serve.

Get ahead: The caramel corn can be made a few days ahead; just store it in an airtight container until ready to use.

CHOCOLATE AND POTATO CHIP PIE

Yield: 1 (9-inch) deep-dish pie **Total time:** 2 hours 30 minutes

A slice of creamy, rich chocolate custard pie is a truly special end to a meal. I wanted to take that classic chocolate custard and put a fun twist on it. Sometimes, the simplest way to do that is to switch out the crust with something . . . unexpected. I introduce to you the Chocolate and Potato Chip Pie. You heard me right, folks: There are potato chips in this pie. In fact, I made a crust with them, and the contrast between the salty potato chips and the decadent chocolate custard is exactly what you need in your life.

Equipment: Food processor, measuring cups or kitchen scale, 9-inch springform pan, saucepan, measuring spoons, mixing bowls, whisk

---

FOR THE POTATO CHIP CRUST

1 (9-ounce) bag salted potato chips (255 grams)

¼ cup flour (32 grams)

1 egg

Nonstick baking spray

TO MAKE THE POTATO CHIP CRUST

1. Preheat the oven to 350°F. Place the chips in a food processor and pulse a few times until the chips are broken down and crumbly. Add the flour and egg and process until combined. Lightly spray a springform pan with nonstick baking spray. Pour the crumb mixture into the springform pan. Press the crumbs down firmly in the bottom and a little up the sides to create the crust. Bake for 12 to 15 minutes, or until the crust is slightly golden brown. Let it cool completely (about 10 minutes while you make the custard).

FOR THE CHOCOLATE CUSTARD FILLING

¾ cup heavy cream
(170 grams)

¾ cup milk
(180 grams)

2 tablespoons
granulated sugar
(25 grams)

1 teaspoon
vanilla extract

¼ teaspoon salt

4 egg yolks

2 tablespoons
cornstarch
(15 grams)

1 cup chocolate chips
(175 grams)

½ teaspoon flaky sea
salt, such as Maldon
or fleur de sel

TO MAKE THE CHOCOLATE CUSTARD FILLING

2. In a small saucepan over medium-high heat, combine the heavy cream, milk, sugar, vanilla, and salt. In a medium bowl, whisk together the egg yolks and cornstarch. In a separate bowl, set aside the chocolate chips. Once the cream mixture is hot, but before it comes to a boil, stream a little of the cream mixture into the egg yolks while whisking. Pour the warmed egg-yolk mixture into the saucepan and continue to cook while whisking until the mixture is thick. Pour the custard over the chocolate chips and let it sit for 1 minute. Stir until the chocolate has fully melted and the custard is smooth. Pour the custard over the cooled crust. Chill in the refrigerator for at least 2 hours. Garnish with flaky sea salt.

Oh no! If your crust is really crumbly when you cut into it, don't worry. Just scoop up the crumbles and garnish the slice with them.

MAPLE-APPLE PIE WITH BACON STREUSEL

Yield: 1 (9-inch) standard pie **Total time:** 4 hours 25 minutes

Maple and bacon are an obvious combination, but when paired with apples and spice, they're elevated to a whole new dimension of flavor. I based the streusel for this pie on the traditional Dutch apple, which replaces the top crust (you can thank me later).

Equipment: Knife, sauté pan, strainer, rolling pin, 9-inch pie plate, peeler, mixing bowls, measuring cups or kitchen scale, measuring spoons, food processor

---

FOR THE CRUST

Single batch All-Butter Crust (page 20)

FOR THE MAPLE-APPLE FILLING

2½ pounds green apples (6 to 7 apples)

¼ cup brown sugar (50 grams)

¼ cup granulated sugar (50 grams)

¼ cup maple syrup (50 grams)

¼ cup cornstarch (30 grams)

½ teaspoon ground cinnamon

1. Prepare a batch of the All-Butter Crust.

2. Dice the bacon for the streusel into small pieces. In a sauté pan over medium heat, cook the bacon until completely crisp. Strain out the bacon pieces and reserve the bacon fat. Freeze the bacon fat until needed and set aside the cooked bacon pieces at room temperature.

3. Preheat the oven to 350°F. Unwrap the disk of dough onto a lightly floured work surface. Lightly flour a rolling pin and begin rolling from the center outward. Roll the dough into a circle roughly 16 inches in diameter. Drape the rolled dough over your rolling pin, then transfer to a pie plate. Trim and crimp the edges. Freeze the piecrust for 10 minutes while preparing the filling.

4. Peel and slice the apples ¼ inch thick. In a large bowl, toss the apple slices with the brown sugar, granulated sugar, maple syrup, cornstarch, cinnamon, allspice, salt, and apple cider vinegar. Pour the filling into the chilled piecrust and bake for 45 minutes. Prepare the streusel during this first bake time.

¼ teaspoon
  ground allspice

½ teaspoon salt

2 tablespoons apple
cider vinegar (28 grams)

FOR THE BACON STREUSEL

5 strips bacon

¼ cup flour
  (32 grams)

¼ cup oats (25 grams)

¼ cup brown sugar
  (50 grams)

2 tablespoons
  unsalted butter
  (28 grams)

¼ teaspoon salt

5. In a food processor, combine the cooked bacon, reserved bacon fat, flour, oats, brown sugar, butter, and salt and pulse until crumbly. Chill in the refrigerator until the streusel is needed.

6. After the first 45-minute bake, sprinkle the streusel over the top of the filling. Bake for an additional 45 minutes. Cool completely at room temperature for at least 2 hours before serving.

More on that: When selecting apples to use for baking, I always go with green Granny Smith apples. They're firm, which means that they hold up well in heat; they're acidic, so the apple flavor comes through even with heavy spices; and they're one of the most accessible types of apple to purchase. If you can't find Granny Smiths, the Jonagold, Honeycrisp, or Pink Lady varieties are all good substitutes.

BLACK-BOTTOM PECAN PIE

Yield: 1 (9-inch) standard pie **Total time:** 1 hour 30 minutes

In my experience, 8 out of 10 people will tell you that their favorite pie is pecan pie. It's a classic: caramel filling with a tender crunch of everyone's favorite nut. And when done right, it has just enough salt to keep you going in for another bite. How can we possibly improve on this already amazing pie? Chocolate. And rum. The black bottom refers to the layer of chocolate underneath the pecan pie filling we already know and love, and the rum just kicks the decadence into high gear. After one bite full of chocolate, caramel, pecan, and rum, you may never want to go back to the plain old classic. And that's okay.

Equipment: Rolling pin, 9-inch pie plate, mixing bowl, measuring cups or kitchen scale, measuring spoons, whisk

---

Single batch Cocoa Crust (page 26)

¾ cup brown sugar (150 grams)

8 tablespoons melted unsalted butter (113 grams)

½ cup dark corn syrup (170 grams)

¼ cup dark rum (85 grams)

2 eggs

1 tablespoon cornstarch (7 grams)

½ teaspoon salt

1 cup chocolate chips (175 grams)

2 cups whole pecans (250 grams)

1. Prepare a batch of the Cocoa Crust.

2. Preheat the oven to 350°F. Unwrap the dough onto a lightly floured work surface. Lightly flour a rolling pin and begin rolling from the center outward. Roll dough into a circle roughly 16 inches in diameter. Drape the dough over your rolling pin, then transfer to a pie plate. Trim and crimp the edges. Freeze the piecrust for 10 minutes.

3. In a medium bowl, combine the brown sugar, melted butter, dark corn syrup, rum, eggs, cornstarch, and salt. Whisk until smooth.

4. Remove the piecrust from the freezer. Place the chocolate chips on top of the dough in an even layer. Pour the liquid filling over the chocolate chips. Arrange the pecans over the filling in an even layer.

5. Bake the pie for 45 minutes, or until the center appears set and does not jiggle. Cool at room temperature before serving.

MAPLE-BUTTERMILK PIE

Yield: 1 (9-inch) standard pie **Total time:** 3 hours 55 minutes

In my first book, *Easy as Pie*, my Buttermilk Pie received so many rave reviews from tasters that I decided to bring it back in this book with an elevated twist. Maple is the perfect sweet element to pair with tangy buttermilk. Combined in a flaky piecrust, these flavors are out of this world. An array of maple leaves cut out of the leftover scraps of dough dress up the pie and make it the perfect treat for your next fall gathering.

Equipment: Rolling pin, 9-inch pie plate, leaf-shaped cookie cutter, sheet pan, parchment paper, mixing bowl, measuring cups or kitchen scale, measuring spoons, whisk

Single batch
All-Butter Crust
(page 20)

1 cup maple syrup
(226 grams)

1 cup buttermilk
(226 grams)

8 tablespoons melted
unsalted butter
(113 grams)

¼ cup granulated
sugar (50 grams)

¼ cup brown sugar
(50 grams)

¼ cup flour (32 grams)

3 eggs

2 tablespoons freshly
squeezed lemon
juice (28 grams)

1 teaspoon
vanilla extract

¾ teaspoon salt

1. Prepare a batch of the All-Butter Crust.

2. Preheat the oven to 400°F. Unwrap the dough onto a lightly floured work surface. Lightly flour a rolling pin and begin rolling from the center outward. Roll the dough into a circle roughly 16 inches in diameter. Drape the dough over your rolling pin, then transfer to a pie plate. Trim and crimp the edges, setting aside the dough scraps to use later. Freeze the piecrust for 10 minutes.

3. Roll out the extra dough and cut out leaf shapes using a cookie cutter, about 5. Place the leaves on a sheet pan lined with parchment paper and bake for 10 minutes, or until golden brown. Set aside.

4. In a large bowl, whisk together the maple syrup, buttermilk, melted butter, granulated sugar, brown sugar, flour, eggs, lemon juice, vanilla, and salt. Pour the filling into the crust and bake for 10 minutes. Reduce the heat to 350°F and bake for an additional 40 minutes. Cool in the refrigerator for at least 2 hours before serving. Garnish the pie with the leaves just before serving.

BANANA CREAM PIE WITH HONEYCOMB CRUNCH

Yield: 1 (9-inch) deep-dish pie **Total time:** 9 hours 45 minutes

I love bananas so much that I had to cut down the number of banana-based desserts in this book. But I think I've nailed it with this one. This pie starts with a buttery crust that's filled with a layer of fresh banana slices, a creamy banana mousse, and a topping of lightly crunchy honeycomb candy pieces. The textural contrast between these layers is to die for. If you're a banana fan like me, you must try this pie.

Equipment: Rolling pin, 9-inch deep-dish pie plate, parchment paper, pie weights, sheet pan, saucepans, measuring cups or kitchen scale, measuring spoons, whisk, mixing bowls, knife, plastic wrap

FOR THE CRUST

Single batch Gluten-Free Crust (page 22), or All-Butter Crust (page 20) if not gluten-free

FOR THE HONEYCOMB CRUNCH

½ cup granulated sugar (100 grams)

¼ cup water

2 tablespoons corn syrup (41 grams)

1 tablespoon honey (21 grams)

1 teaspoon baking soda

TO BLIND-BAKE THE CRUST

1. Prepare a batch of the Gluten-Free Crust or All-Butter Crust.

2. Preheat the oven to 375°F. Unwrap the dough onto a lightly floured work surface. Lightly flour a rolling pin and begin rolling from the center outward. Roll the dough into a circle roughly 16 inches in diameter. Drape the dough over your rolling pin, then transfer to a deep-dish pie plate. Trim and crimp the edges. Freeze the piecrust for 10 minutes.

3. Remove the piecrust from the freezer. Lay a large piece of parchment paper over the center of the dish and fill with pie weights. Blind-bake in the preheated oven for 20 minutes. Remove the weights and bake for an additional 15 minutes. Cool completely at room temperature (about 15 minutes while you make the honeycomb and prep the bananas).

continued >

FOR THE FRESH BANANA LAYER

2 bananas, sliced

1 tablespoon freshly squeezed lemon juice (14 grams)

FOR THE BANANA MOUSSE

½ cup mashed banana (from 1 small banana)

¼ cup cornstarch (30 grams)

4 egg yolks

1 cup heavy cream (226 grams)

1 cup milk (226 grams)

½ cup granulated sugar (100 grams)

1 teaspoon vanilla extract

¼ teaspoon salt

2 tablespoons cold unsalted butter (28 grams)

TO MAKE THE HONEYCOMB CRUNCH

4. Line a sheet pan with parchment paper. In a small saucepan, combine the sugar, water, corn syrup, and honey over high heat. When the sugar has cooked down and begins to turn amber, quickly remove from the heat and whisk in the baking soda. The mixture will bubble up fiercely. Quickly pour the mixture onto the lined pan and let it cool at room temperature for 1 hour. Break into small pieces with a knife and store in an airtight container.

TO MAKE THE FRESH BANANA LAYER

5. In a medium bowl, toss the sliced bananas in lemon juice. Line the bottom of the cooled piecrust with the banana slices.

TO MAKE THE BANANA MOUSSE

6. In a medium bowl, combine the mashed banana, cornstarch, and egg yolks and whisk until smooth. In a medium saucepan, combine the heavy cream, milk, sugar, vanilla, and salt over medium-high heat. Once the cream mixture is hot, stream a little of it into the egg-yolk mixture while whisking to heat up the egg yolks. Pour the warmed egg-yolk mixture into the saucepan and cook while whisking until thick. Remove from the heat and whisk in the cold butter until smooth. Pour the banana mousse over the banana slices. Cover the surface with plastic wrap and chill in the refrigerator for at least 8 hours before serving.

7. To serve, top the pie with the honeycomb crunch.

CHOCOLATE-PUMPKIN PIE WITH DULCE DE LECHE SWIRL

Yield: 1 (9-inch) deep-dish pie **Total time:** 5 hours 40 minutes

It's a travesty to go without pumpkin pie on Thanksgiving. But why not try to spruce it up a little? This twist features a light, no-bake custard that is swirled into a Cocoa Crust with dulce de leche and chocolate ganache. The beautiful marbled design will impress just as much as the flavor.

Equipment: Rolling pin, 9-inch deep-dish pie plate, parchment paper, pie weights, mixing bowls, measuring cups or kitchen scale, measuring spoons, microwave-safe bowls, piping bags, whisk, saucepan, toothpick

FOR THE CRUST

Single batch Cocoa Crust (page 26)

FOR THE DULCE DE LECHE SAUCE

1 tablespoon cold water

½ teaspoon gelatin powder

½ cup dulce de leche (160 grams)

TO BLIND-BAKE THE CRUST

1. Prepare a batch of the Cocoa Crust.

2. Preheat the oven to 375°F. Unwrap the dough onto a lightly floured work surface. Lightly flour a rolling pin and begin rolling from the center outward. Roll the dough into a circle roughly 16 inches in diameter. Drape the dough over your rolling pin, then transfer to a deep-dish pie plate. Trim and crimp the edges. Freeze the piecrust for 10 minutes.

3. Remove the piecrust from the freezer. Lay a large piece of parchment paper over the center of the dish and fill with pie weights. Blind-bake in the preheated oven for 20 minutes. Remove the weights and bake for an additional 15 minutes. Cool completely at room temperature (about 15 minutes while you continue the recipe).

continued >

FOR THE CHOCOLATE GANACHE

2 tablespoons chocolate chips (28 grams)

2 tablespoons heavy cream (28 grams)

FOR THE PUMPKIN MOUSSE

¼ cup cold water

1 tablespoon gelatin powder (9 grams)

2 eggs, separated

½ cup granulated sugar, divided (100 grams)

1 (15-ounce) can pumpkin puree (425 grams)

1 teaspoon vanilla extract

1 teaspoon ground cinnamon

½ teaspoon ground ginger

⅛ teaspoon ground allspice

TO MAKE THE DULCE DE LECHE SAUCE

4. In a small bowl, combine the cold water and gelatin powder and set aside to let bloom. In a microwave-safe bowl, heat the dulce de leche for 30 seconds in the microwave. Mix the bloomed gelatin into the dulce de leche until smooth. Transfer to a piping bag and set aside.

TO MAKE THE CHOCOLATE GANACHE

5. In a microwave-safe bowl, heat the chocolate chips and heavy cream together in a microwave in 30-second increments until melted. Mix until smooth. Transfer to a piping bag and set aside.

TO MAKE THE PUMPKIN MOUSSE

6. In a small bowl, combine the cold water and gelatin powder and set aside to let bloom. In a medium bowl, combine the egg whites and ¼ cup of sugar (50 grams) and whisk until stiff peaks form. Set aside. In a medium saucepan, combine the pumpkin puree, remaining ¼ cup of sugar (50 grams), egg yolks, vanilla, cinnamon, ginger, and allspice. Set over medium-high heat and whisk until it starts to bubble, then continue whisking over the heat for 3 minutes. Remove from the heat and mix in the bloomed gelatin until smooth, then fold into the whipped egg whites. Pour the pumpkin mousse into the cooled piecrust.

7. Pipe the dulce de leche into the pumpkin mousse in lines. Pipe the chocolate ganache over the top, also in lines. Use a toothpick to swirl the fillings together to create a marbled design. Chill the pie in the refrigerator for at least 4 hours before serving.

More on that: If you can't find dulce de leche in stores, you can easily make it at home. Get a can of sweetened condensed milk and boil the can in water for 4 hours to caramelize it. The water will evaporate while boiling, so you will have to keep refilling it. Make sure the can is submerged at a rapid boil throughout this time. Cool the can completely at room temperature before opening to reveal your dulce de leche.

SOUR CREAM CHEESECAKE WITH SOUR CHERRY COMPOTE

Yield: 1 (9-inch) cheesecake **Total time:** 4 hours 45 minutes

Cherry cheesecake is a classic dessert that screams summer to me. I decided to put a spin on the traditional dessert by using sour cream in place of cream cheese. The lightly sweetened sour cream mousse pairs beautifully with a sour cherry compote. Plus, you'll only need to turn your oven on for 10 minutes, making this refreshing pie the perfect choice for a hot summer day.

Equipment: Food processor, measuring cups or kitchen scale, measuring spoons, 9-inch springform pan, mixing bowls, saucepans, whisk, spatula

FOR THE GRAHAM CRACKER CRUST

2 cups graham cracker crumbs, from 12 sheets of crackers (170 grams)

¼ cup granulated sugar (50 grams)

¼ teaspoon salt

8 tablespoons melted unsalted butter (113 grams)

Nonstick baking spray

FOR THE SOUR CREAM CHEESECAKE FILLING

¼ cup cold water

1 tablespoon gelatin powder (9 grams)

TO MAKE THE GRAHAM CRACKER CRUST

1. Preheat the oven to 350°F. In a food processor, combine the graham cracker crumbs, sugar, and salt. Stream in the melted butter. Pulse until all crumbs are wet. Lightly spray a springform pan with nonstick baking spray. Pour the graham cracker mixture into the springform pan. Press the crumbs down firmly in the bottom and up the sides to create the crust. Bake for 10 minutes. Let the piecrust cool completely at room temperature (about 10 minutes while you make the filling).

TO MAKE THE SOUR CREAM CHEESECAKE FILLING

2. In a small bowl, combine the cold water and gelatin powder and set aside to let bloom. In a small saucepan over medium-high heat, mix together the sugar and ½ cup of heavy cream (113 grams). In another bowl, set aside the sour cream. In a medium bowl, whisk the remaining 1 cup of heavy cream (226 grams) until stiff peaks form. Set aside. When the first cream mixture is hot, whisk in the bloomed gelatin. Pour the mixture over the sour

1 cup granulated
  sugar (200 grams)

1½ cups heavy cream,
  divided (339 grams)

2 cups sour cream
  (1 pound,
  454 grams)

**FOR THE SOUR
CHERRY COMPOTE**

2 pounds (4 cups)
  fresh or frozen
  pitted cherries

⅓ cup granulated
  sugar (68 grams)

2 tablespoons freshly
  squeezed lemon
  juice (28 grams)

1 tablespoon
  cornstarch (7 grams)

¼ teaspoon pectin

cream and whisk until smooth. Fold the whipped cream into the sour cream mixture until fully combined. Pour the filling into the cooled crust. Chill in the refrigerator for at least 2 hours.

TO MAKE THE SOUR CHERRY COMPOTE

3. In a large saucepan, combine the cherries, sugar, lemon juice, cornstarch, and pectin and toss with a spatula to coat. Place over high heat and cook, stirring frequently, for 20 minutes, or until thickened. Let the compote cool at room temperature for 10 minutes, then pour over the sour cream cheesecake filling. Smooth out evenly with a spatula. Chill in the refrigerator for at least 2 hours before serving.

Fancy it up: Some say that crème fraîche is the French version of sour cream. It is similar in taste and can give your dish a boost of richness. Just swap in an equal amount of crème fraîche for the sour cream to make an even more decadent pie.

PUMPKIN AND CHÈVRE CHEESECAKE WITH BROWN BUTTER GRAHAM CRUST

Yield: 1 (9-inch) cheesecake **Total time:** 1 hour 30 minutes

I first tested this recipe as a trial dessert menu option in one of my restaurants a few years ago. It was such a hit that I decided to make it for my family's Thanksgiving dinner. Although a little wary at first, the family absolutely approved, and it's been in rotation ever since. Move over pumpkin cheesecake—there's a new cheesecake in town. Your wonderful tanginess just does not compare to the even tangier tanginess that only goat cheese can provide. And to make it that much more decadent, it's sitting on top of a brown butter graham crust.

Equipment: Saucepan, measuring cups or kitchen scale, food processor, measuring spoons, 9-inch springform pan, stand mixer with paddle attachment, spatula

FOR THE CRUST

10 tablespoons unsalted butter (141 grams)

2 cups graham cracker crumbs, crushed from 12 sheets of crackers (170 grams)

¼ cup brown sugar (50 grams)

¼ teaspoon salt

Nonstick baking spray

TO MAKE THE CRUST

1. Preheat the oven to 350°F. In a small saucepan over medium heat, heat the butter until it has fully melted and the milk solids start to caramelize. The butter will start to turn foamy and smell nutty. Remove from heat and set aside.

2. In a food processor, mix the graham cracker crumbs, brown sugar, and salt. Stream in the browned butter and mix to combine. Lightly spray a springform pan with nonstick baking spray. Pour the graham cracker mixture into the springform pan and press firmly in the bottom and up the sides to create a crust. Bake the crust for 10 minutes.

FOR THE FILLING

1 (15-ounce) can
pumpkin puree

1½ cups goat
cheese (12 ounces,
340 grams)

½ cup granulated
sugar (100 grams)

½ cup brown sugar
(100 grams)

¼ cup cornstarch
(30 grams)

½ cup sour cream
(113 grams)

¾ teaspoon
ground cinnamon

¾ teaspoon
ground ginger

¼ teaspoon
ground cloves

¼ teaspoon
ground nutmeg

4 eggs

TO MAKE THE FILLING

3. In a stand mixer fitted with a paddle attachment, combine the pumpkin and goat cheese. Mix in the granulated sugar, brown sugar, and cornstarch, then add the sour cream. Scrape down the sides as needed. Add the cinnamon, ginger, cloves, and nutmeg, and, finally, the eggs.

4. Pour the filling on top of the baked crust. Reduce the oven to 275°F and bake for 1 hour, or until the filling is set in the middle and does not appear liquid. Cool for 4 hours before serving.

More on that: When buying goat cheese for this recipe, the plain goat cheese that comes in a log is the best way go to. It's creamier and mixes wonderfully when creating this filling.

White Peach Twisted Lattice Pie with Herbed Crust, page 62

CHAPTER 4

Nutty, Creamy, and Other Sweet Pies

This chapter is all about my favorite flavors transformed into pie. I reimagined some nostalgic desserts and also dreamed up entirely new combinations.

WHITE PEACH TWISTED LATTICE PIE WITH HERBED CRUST

Yield: 1 (9-inch) standard pie **Total time:** 4 hours 25 minutes

My all-time favorite pie is a peach pie. It was introduced to me by my grandmother, who had a peach tree in her backyard. I fell in love with the flavor and asked for a peach pie in lieu of a birthday cake for many years. In this recipe, I've used white peaches for their subtle sweet flavor and paired them with my herby whole wheat crust. I promise this flavor combination is a worthy twist on the classic.

Equipment: Peeler, knife, mixing bowls, measuring cups or kitchen scale, measuring spoons, whisk, rolling pin, 9-inch pie plate, pastry brush, pastry wheel

---

Double batch Whole Wheat Crust with Thyme (page 24)

2½ pounds white peaches (about 8 white peaches)

¾ cup granulated sugar (150 grams)

¼ cup cornstarch (30 grams)

2 tablespoons freshly squeezed lemon juice (28 grams)

1 tablespoon grated lemon zest

½ teaspoon vanilla extract

½ teaspoon salt

1 egg

2 tablespoons water

1. Prepare a double batch of the Whole Wheat Crust with Thyme.

2. Peel and slice the white peaches ¼ inch thick and put the slices in a large bowl. Add the sugar, cornstarch, lemon juice, lemon zest, vanilla, and salt and toss until the peaches are evenly coated.

3. In a small bowl, whisk together the egg and water to make an egg wash. Set aside until needed.

4. Unwrap one disk of dough onto a lightly floured work surface. Lightly flour a rolling pin and begin rolling from the center outward. Roll the dough into a circle roughly 16 inches in diameter. Drape the dough over your rolling pin, then transfer to a pie plate. Leave the edges hanging over the dish for now. Fill the crust with the peach filling. Use a pastry brush to brush some of the egg wash around the edges of the crust and set aside the remaining egg wash.

5. Preheat the oven to 350°F. Unwrap the other disk of dough onto a lightly floured work surface. Lightly flour a rolling pin and begin rolling

from the center outward. Roll the dough into a 12-by-18-inch rectangle. Use a knife or a pastry wheel to cut 10 strips ¼ inch thick. Cut out 5 (1-inch) strips from the rest of the dough.

6. With the thinner strips, take 2 strips at a time and twist them together. Do this with all of the thinner strips, creating 5 twists. Arrange the 5 thicker strips over the filled pie from top to bottom. Take every other strip and fold it from the bottom to the top. Lay one twist down horizontally toward the top of the pie, then fold the first 2 strips back down. Continue to do this, alternating strips and twists each time, until you have 5 vertical strips and 5 horizontal twists. Trim the edges to extend ½ inch over the side of the pie plate. Roll up the overhanging dough to form a crust around the edge of the pie plate. Brush the remaining egg wash over the entire pie. Freeze the pie for 10 minutes before baking.

7. Bake the pie for 1 hour 30 minutes. Cool at room temperature for at least 2 hours before serving.

Fancy it up: To make even more of a showstopping pie, use a cookie cutter to cut out fun shapes from any extra scraps of dough. Apply the shapes with egg wash to the top of the lattice before brushing the entire pie with the remaining egg wash.

CRANBERRY-ORANGE CUSTARD PIE

Yield: 1 (9-inch) standard pie **Total time:** 5 hours

When I was younger, I never understood the idea of serving cranberry sauce at Thanksgiving. It seemed weird that a jam was being served with turkey. But the more I tried it, the more I loved it. My mom made the best cranberry sauce with a hint of orange, and this pie is an interpretation of that. It's a little tart with a burst of sweet orange flavor mixed in. Delicious.

Equipment: Food processor, measuring cups or kitchen scale, measuring spoons, 9-inch pie plate, knife, mixing bowls, blender, saucepan, metal bowl, whisk, spatula, microwave-safe bowl, sheet pan, cooling rack, zester

FOR THE GRAHAM CRACKER CRUST

2 cups graham cracker crumbs, from 12 sheets of crackers (170 grams)

¼ cup granulated sugar (50 grams)

¼ teaspoon salt

8 tablespoons melted unsalted butter (113 grams)

Nonstick baking spray

FOR THE CRANBERRY-ORANGE FILLING

8 tablespoons cold unsalted butter (113 grams)

1 cup fresh cranberries, or ½ cup cranberry puree (113 grams)

TO MAKE THE GRAHAM CRACKER CRUST

1. Preheat the oven to 350°F. In a food processor, combine the graham cracker crumbs, sugar, and salt. Stream in the melted butter. Pulse until all crumbs are wet. Lightly spray a pie plate with nonstick baking spray. Pour the graham cracker mixture into the pie plate. Press the crumbs down firmly in the bottom and up the sides to create the crust. Bake for 10 minutes. Let the crust cool at room temperature while preparing the filling.

TO MAKE THE CRANBERRY-ORANGE FILLING

2. Cube the cold butter and set it aside. In a blender, combine the fresh cranberries and orange juice and puree. Heat a saucepan with 2 cups of water to simmer. In a metal bowl set over the saucepan, combine the juice mixture, sugar, eggs, egg yolk, lemon juice, and orange zest. Whisk until the custard has lightened in color and doubled in size. Once the custard is cooked, remove from the heat and whisk in the cold butter. Once the butter is fully incorporated, pour the custard into the crust and smooth it out with a spatula. Chill for at least 4 hours.

¼ cup freshly squeezed
   orange juice
   (56 grams)

¼ cup granulated sugar
   (50 grams)

2 eggs

1 egg yolk

1 tablespoon freshly
   squeezed lemon juice
   (14 grams)

1 tablespoon grated
   orange zest

FOR THE CANDIED CRANBERRIES

3 tablespoons
   granulated sugar,
   divided (38 grams)

1 tablespoon water

¼ cup fresh cranberries
   (28 grams)

1 orange

TO MAKE THE CANDIED CRANBERRIES

3. In a microwave-safe bowl, heat 1 tablespoon of sugar (13 grams) and the water in the microwave in 30-second increments until the sugar has dissolved into the water. In a small bowl, set aside the remaining 2 tablespoons of sugar (25 grams). Line a sheet pan with a cooling rack. Coat the fresh cranberries in the simple syrup, then roll in the sugar. Place the coated cranberries on the cooling rack to air dry, about 1 hour.

4. To garnish, place the candied cranberries around the pie. Use a zester to peel strips of orange rind and sprinkle over the pie.

More on that: If you can't find fresh cranberries, you can use the same amount of canned cranberry sauce. Just don't use the jellied kind.

APRICOT, PLUM, AND PEACH PIE WITH PISTACHIO FRANGIPANE

Yield: 1 (9-inch) deep-dish pie **Total time:** 4 hours 30 minutes

Stone-fruit season is my favorite season. I get so excited when I see these pretty little fruits begin to show up in my grocery store. This pie is all about my love for stone fruit, but to spruce it up even more, I added in a layer of crunchy pistachio frangipane for extra flavor and a hint of color. A clean slice of this pie will show the marbled reds and oranges of the fruit lined with a toasty green bottom layer.

Equipment: Food processor, measuring cups or kitchen scale, measuring spoons, knife, mixing bowls, rolling pin, 9-inch deep-dish pie plate, whisk, pastry brush

FOR THE CRUST

Double batch
  All-Butter Crust
  (page 20)

2 tablespoons water

1 egg

FOR THE PISTACHIO FRANGIPANE

½ cup toasted
  pistachios
  (50 grams)

¼ cup granulated
  sugar (50 grams)

3 tablespoons melted
  unsalted butter
  (42 grams)

2 egg yolks

1 tablespoon flour
  (9 grams)

¼ teaspoon salt

TO MAKE THE CRUST

1. Prepare a double batch of the All-Butter Crust.

TO MAKE THE PISTACHIO FRANGIPANE

2. In a food processor mix the pistachios, sugar, melted butter, egg yolks, flour, and salt. Mix until smooth, though some chunks of pistachio are okay. Set aside until needed.

TO MAKE THE FILLING

3. Slice the apricots, plums, and peaches ¼ inch thick and put them in a large bowl. Add the cornstarch, granulated sugar, brown sugar, lemon juice, and salt and toss until everything is evenly coated.

4. Unwrap one disk of dough onto a lightly floured work surface. Lightly flour a rolling pin and begin rolling from the center outward. Roll the dough into a circle roughly 16 inches in diameter. Drape the dough over your rolling pin, then transfer to a deep-dish pie plate. Trim the edges.

FOR THE FILLING

2½ pounds apricots, plums, and peaches

¼ cup cornstarch (30 grams)

¼ cup granulated sugar (50 grams)

½ cup brown sugar (100 grams)

2 tablespoons freshly squeezed lemon juice (28 grams)

¼ teaspoon salt

5. Fill the crust with the pistachio frangipane first, smoothing it out in an even layer. Top with the fruit filling. In a small bowl, whisk together the water and egg to make an egg wash. Use a pastry brush to brush egg wash around the edges of the dough and set aside the remaining egg wash.

6. Preheat the oven to 350°F. Unwrap the other disk of dough onto a lightly floured flat work surface. Lightly flour a rolling pin and begin rolling from the center outward. Roll the dough into a circle roughly 16 inches in diameter. Drape the dough over your rolling pin, then lay it over the top of the pie. Trim and crimp the edges. Apply the remaining egg wash around the surface of the pie. Freeze the pie for 10 minutes.

7. Use a knife to cut an *X* in the top crust. Cut 4 more slits around the pie to vent. Bake the pie for 1 hour 30 minutes. Cool at room temperature for at least 2 hours before serving.

Fancy it up: You can use the second crust to create a beautiful lattice design instead of a top crust. Try twists, braids, or a fluted strip to give your pie some extra pizzazz.

TANGERINE AND OLIVE OIL PIE WITH TOASTED ALMONDS

Yield: 1 (9-inch) standard pie **Total time:** 5 hours 35 minutes

The sour tanginess of a tangerine and the fruity notes of olive oil are a match made in heaven. For this recipe, I've put a simple twist on an orange curd. Instead of mounting with butter, olive oil is emulsified into the custard. The texture is light and the flavor is perfect for any time of the year.

Equipment: Rolling pin, 9-inch pie plate, parchment paper, pie weights, sheet pan, measuring cups or kitchen scale, measuring spoons, mixing bowl, saucepan, metal bowl, whisk

---

Single batch Cornmeal Crust (page 25)

¼ cup sliced almonds (30 grams)

1 tablespoon cold water

1 teaspoon gelatin powder

½ cup freshly squeezed tangerine juice (120 grams)

¼ cup sugar (50 grams)

3 eggs

2 tablespoons freshly squeezed lemon juice (28 grams)

Grated zest of 1 lemon

¼ teaspoon salt

¼ cup olive oil (56 grams)

1. Prepare a batch of the Cornmeal Crust.

2. Preheat the oven to 375°F. Unwrap the dough onto a lightly floured work surface. Lightly flour a rolling pin and begin rolling from the center outward. Roll the dough into a circle roughly 16 inches in diameter. Drape the dough over your rolling pin, then transfer to a pie plate. Trim and crimp the edges. Freeze the piecrust for 10 minutes.

3. Remove the piecrust from the freezer. Lay a large piece of parchment paper over the center of the dish and fill with pie weights. Blind-bake in the preheated oven for 20 minutes. Remove the weights and bake for an additional 15 minutes. Cool completely at room temperature (about 15 minutes while you continue the recipe).

4. On a sheet pan in the oven, toast the sliced almonds for 5 minutes, or until golden brown. Cool completely at room temperature.

5. In a small bowl, combine the cold water and gelatin powder and set aside to let bloom. Prepare a double boiler by heating a saucepan with 2 cups of water to a simmer. In a metal bowl, combine the tangerine juice, sugar, eggs, lemon juice, lemon zest, and salt. Whisk until combined and place over the simmering water. Whisk continuously until the mixture has thickened, doubled in size, and lightened in color. Stream in the olive oil a little at a time while whisking to emulsify the olive oil. Remove from the heat and add the bloomed gelatin. Stir until the gelatin has fully dissolved. Pour the custard into the piecrust and chill in the refrigerator for at least 4 hours.

6. To garnish, top the pie with the toasted almonds.

> **Don't have that?** Tangerines are not always in season, so if you can't find them, you can select any variety of orange you'd like. Blood oranges, mandarin oranges, Cara Cara oranges, and other navel oranges are all great options.

MILK AND COOKIES ICEBOX PIE WITH CHOCOLATE COOKIE CRUST

Yield: 1 (9-inch) deep-dish pie **Total time:** 55 minutes

Let's be honest. After a hard day at work, you just want to go home and pour yourself a tall glass of . . . cold milk to dunk your cookies in. Or is that just me? This pie has everything you love in that simple combination of cookies and milk. A homemade chocolate chip cookie butter sits on top of a chocolate sandwich cookie crust, and it's all topped with a milky whipped cream. You may still need that tall glass of milk to wash down this rich pie, though.

Equipment: Food processor, 9-inch deep-dish pie plate, mixing bowls, measuring cups or kitchen scale, measuring spoons, sheet pan, parchment paper, whisk, stand mixer with paddle attachment and whisk attachment, spatula, piping bag

FOR THE CHOCOLATE SANDWICH COOKIE CRUST

24 chocolate
   sandwich cookies

5 tablespoons melted
   unsalted butter
   (71 grams)

¼ teaspoon salt

Nonstick baking spray

FOR THE CHOCOLATE CHIP COOKIE BUTTER

½ cup flour
   (64 grams)

¼ cup brown sugar
   (50 grams)

TO MAKE THE CHOCOLATE SANDWICH COOKIE CRUST

1. In a food processor, pulse the chocolate sandwich cookies, melted butter, and salt into crumbs. Lightly spray a deep-dish pie plate with nonstick baking spray. Pour the crumbs into the pie plate and press them down firmly in the bottom and up the sides to create the crust. Chill in the refrigerator until ready to use.

TO MAKE THE CHOCOLATE CHIP COOKIE BUTTER

2. Preheat the oven to 350°F. In a medium bowl, combine the flour, brown sugar, melted butter, egg, granulated sugar, vanilla, salt, baking soda, and baking powder and mix well. Mix in the chocolate chips. Line a sheet pan with parchment paper and scoop the cookie dough onto the pan by the tablespoon. Bake the cookies for 8 to 10 minutes. Let the cookies cool completely at room temperature (about 10 minutes while you continue the recipe).

continued >

2 tablespoons melted
unsalted butter
(28 grams)

1 egg

1 tablespoon granulated
sugar (13 grams)

½ teaspoon vanilla extract

¼ teaspoon salt

⅛ teaspoon baking soda

⅛ teaspoon
baking powder

¼ cup chocolate chips
(36 grams)

1 cup heavy cream
(226 grams)

1 (8-ounce) package
cream cheese
(226 grams)

½ cup confectioners'
sugar (60 grams)

FOR THE MILKY
WHIPPED CREAM

1 cup heavy cream
(226 grams)

½ cup confectioners'
sugar (60 grams)

¼ cup milk powder
(30 grams)

3. In a large bowl, whisk the heavy cream until stiff peaks form. Set aside. In a stand mixer fitted with a paddle attachment, mix the cream cheese and confectioners' sugar. Add the cooled chocolate chip cookies and turn on low, letting the paddle attachment crush the cookies into the cream cheese mixture. Scrape down the sides as needed. Some cookie chunks are okay. Fold the cookie mixture into the whipped cream until no white streaks remain. Pour the filling into the crust and smooth out with a spatula. Chill in the refrigerator while preparing the topping.

TO MAKE THE MILKY WHIPPED CREAM

4. Mix the heavy cream, confectioners' sugar, and milk powder in a stand mixer fitted with a whisk attachment. Whip until stiff peaks form. Use a piping bag to pipe the topping onto the filling, or smooth it on with a spatula.

Get ahead: The chocolate chip cookies can be made up to a week in advance. Prepare as directed and store in an airtight container at room temperature until ready to use.

IRISH SLAMMER ICEBOX PIE WITH WHISKEY CARAMEL

Yield: 1 (9-inch) deep-dish pie **Total time:** 7 hours

Who remembers younger years when you would down Irish Slammers with your friends? You quickly drop the shot glass filled with Irish cream and whiskey into a full, cold glass of dark stout and drink it as fast as you can before it curdles. It mixes into a bitter, caramel-y, delicious drink, and I wanted to recreate that combination for this pie. We may not down Irish Slammers regularly these days, but we can still enjoy the flavors in this pie. I've mixed the stout with a chocolate custard and layered on a whiskey caramel and an Irish cream whipped topping. No need to chug; just get your forks ready.

Equipment: Food processor, measuring cups or kitchen scale, measuring spoons, 9-inch deep-dish pie plate, mixing bowls, whisk, saucepans, plastic wrap, spatula, stand mixer with whisk attachment

---

FOR THE GRAHAM CRACKER CRUST

2 cups graham cracker crumbs, from 12 sheets of crackers (170 grams)

¼ cup granulated sugar (50 grams)

¼ teaspoon salt

8 tablespoons melted unsalted butter (113 grams)

Nonstick baking spray

TO MAKE THE GRAHAM CRACKER CRUST

1. Preheat the oven to 350°F. In a food processor, combine the graham cracker crumbs, sugar, and salt. Stream in the melted butter. Pulse until all crumbs are wet. Lightly spray a deep-dish pie plate with nonstick baking spray. Pour the graham cracker mixture into the pie plate. Press the crumbs down firmly in the bottom and up the sides to create the crust. Bake for 10 minutes, then let cool at room temperature.

continued >

FOR THE CHOCOLATE-STOUT CUSTARD

1 cup chocolate chips (175 grams)

4 egg yolks

2 tablespoons cornstarch (15 grams)

1 cup heavy cream (226 grams)

½ cup stout (120 grams)

⅓ cup granulated sugar (68 grams)

¼ teaspoon salt

FOR THE WHISKEY CARAMEL

½ cup heavy cream (113 grams)

3 tablespoons unsalted butter (42 grams)

⅛ teaspoon salt

¾ cup granulated sugar (150 grams)

2 tablespoons whiskey (28 grams)

2 tablespoons water

TO MAKE THE CHOCOLATE-STOUT CUSTARD

2. In a medium bowl, set aside the chocolate chips. In another bowl, whisk the egg yolks and cornstarch together and set aside. In a small saucepan over medium-high heat, combine the heavy cream, stout, sugar, and salt. Once hot, stream a little into the egg yolks while whisking. Pour the egg-yolk mixture into the saucepan and cook until thick, then immediately pour over the chocolate and whisk until smooth. Pour the custard into the cooled crust. Place a piece of plastic wrap over the surface of the custard and chill in the refrigerator for at least 4 hours.

TO MAKE THE WHISKEY CARAMEL

3. In a small saucepan over medium-high heat, heat the heavy cream, butter, and salt until melted together. In another saucepan over medium-high heat, combine the sugar, whiskey, and water and heat until the sugar dissolves and the mixture appears amber in color. Do not stir during this time. Once the sugar has turned amber, remove from the heat and whisk in the cream mixture a little at a time. The sugar will bubble up, so be careful. Continue to whisk in the cream mixture until fully incorporated. Pour the caramel over the chilled custard and smooth it out with a spatula. Chill in the refrigerator for at least 2 hours.

FOR THE IRISH CREAM WHIPPED TOPPING

1 cup heavy cream (226 grams)

⅓ cup confectioners' sugar (40 grams)

2 tablespoons Irish cream liqueur (28 grams)

TO MAKE THE IRISH CREAM WHIPPED TOPPING

4. In the bowl of a stand mixer fitted with a whisk attachment, combine the heavy cream and confectioners' sugar. Whip until stiff peaks form. Add the Irish cream and mix until incorporated. Top the pie with the Irish cream whipped topping and smooth it out with a spatula.

Oh no! If you're afraid your custard is about to curdle, immediately throw it in a blender and blend until smooth. This can usually save your custard.

Get ahead: You can make the crust, custard, and caramel several days in advance, layer them in the piecrust, and keep in the refrigerator for up to a week. When you're ready to serve, finish the pie with the Irish cream whipped topping.

OATMEAL-RAISIN-COOKIE PIE WITH MARSHMALLOW MERINGUE

Yield: 1 (9-inch) standard pie **Total time:** 1 hour 35 minutes

One of my favorite cookies is an oatmeal cream cookie. It's chewy, pull-apart gooey, and all things delicious. This dessert has all the goodness of an oatmeal cream cookie–but in an actual pie. I use old-fashioned rolled oats in this filling, which bake up into a super chewy, caramel-y, all-things-delicious pie.

Equipment: Rolling pin, 9-inch pie plate, mixing bowls, measuring cups or kitchen scale, measuring spoons, whisk, saucepan, metal bowl, stand mixer with whisk attachment, spatula

---

FOR THE CRUST

Single batch All-Butter Crust (page 20)

FOR THE OATMEAL-RAISIN FILLING

¾ cup brown sugar (150 grams)

½ cup dark corn syrup (170 grams)

8 tablespoons melted unsalted butter (113 grams)

2 eggs

1 tablespoon cornstarch (7 grams)

½ teaspoon salt

1 cup rolled oats (90 grams)

½ cup raisins (75 grams)

TO MAKE THE CRUST

1. Prepare a batch of the All-Butter Crust.

2. Preheat the oven to 350°F. Unwrap the dough onto a lightly floured work surface. Lightly flour a rolling pin and begin rolling from the center outward. Roll the dough into a circle roughly 16 inches in diameter. Drape the dough over your rolling pin, then transfer to a pie plate. Trim and crimp the edges. Freeze the piecrust for 10 minutes.

TO MAKE THE OATMEAL-RAISIN FILLING

3. In a medium bowl, combine the brown sugar, dark corn syrup, melted butter, eggs, cornstarch, and salt. Whisk until smooth. Mix in the rolled oats and raisins, then pour the filling into the chilled piecrust. Bake for 45 minutes, or until the center appears set and not liquid. Chill the pie in the refrigerator for 1 hour.

FOR THE MARSHMALLOW MERINGUE

1 cup granulated sugar (200 grams)

3 egg whites

½ teaspoon vanilla paste or ¼ vanilla bean pod

4. Prepare a double boiler by setting a saucepan filled with 2 cups of water over low heat until it reaches a simmer. In a metal bowl, whisk the sugar and egg whites over the simmering water until the sugar dissolves and the egg whites are warm to the touch. Transfer the egg white mixture to a stand mixer fitted with a whisk attachment and whip until stiff peaks form. Add the vanilla and mix again. Top the pie with the meringue and use a spatula to distribute to all the edges. Chill in the refrigerator until ready to serve.

Don't have that? You can turn this recipe into an Oatmeal-Chocolate-Chip-Cookie Pie by replacing the raisins with chocolate chips.

BLACK FOREST CREAM PIE

Yield: 1 (9-inch) deep-dish pie **Total time:** 7 hours, plus 8 hours to chill

I've stacked up four amazing layers of goodness in this pie interpretation of a Black Forest cake. It starts with a flaky Cocoa Crust base, followed by a creamy no-bake chocolate custard, set with a sour cherry jam filling, and topped with a white chocolate whipped ganache. This pie will keep you going back bite after bite.

Equipment: Microwave-safe bowl, measuring cups or kitchen scale, plastic wrap, rolling pin, 9-inch deep-dish pie plate, parchment paper, pie weights, mixing bowls, saucepan, measuring spoons, food processor, spatula, stand mixer with whisk attachment

FOR THE WHITE CHOCOLATE WHIPPED GANACHE

1 cup heavy cream, divided (226 grams)

1 cup white chocolate chips (144 grams)

FOR THE CRUST

Single batch Cocoa Crust (page 26)

TO MAKE THE WHITE CHOCOLATE WHIPPED GANACHE

1. In a microwave-safe bowl, microwave ½ cup of heavy cream (113 grams) and the white chocolate chips until melted. Cool the white chocolate ganache in the refrigerator. Once cooled, cover with plastic wrap and chill overnight.

TO BLIND-BAKE THE CRUST

2. Prepare a batch of the Cocoa Crust.

3. Preheat the oven to 375°F. Unwrap the dough onto a lightly floured work surface. Lightly flour a rolling pin and begin rolling from the center outward. Roll the dough into a circle roughly 16 inches in diameter. Drape the dough over your rolling pin, then transfer to a deep-dish pie plate. Trim and crimp the edges. Freeze the piecrust for 10 minutes.

4. Remove the piecrust from the freezer. Lay a large piece of parchment paper over the center of the dish and fill with pie weights. Blind-bake in the preheated oven for 20 minutes. Remove the weights and bake for an additional 15 minutes. Cool completely at room temperature (about 15 minutes while you make the custard).

FOR THE CHOCOLATE CUSTARD

1 cup heavy cream (226 grams)

1 cup milk (226 grams)

2 tablespoons granulated sugar (25 grams)

2 tablespoons cocoa powder (15 grams)

1 teaspoon vanilla extract

¼ teaspoon salt

4 egg yolks

2 tablespoons cornstarch (15 grams)

4 ounces dark chocolate, chopped (113 grams)

FOR THE CHERRY JAM

2 cups pitted fresh or frozen cherries (1 pound, 450 grams)

⅓ cup granulated sugar (68 grams)

2 tablespoons freshly squeezed lemon juice (28 grams)

1 teaspoon pectin

TO MAKE THE CHOCOLATE CUSTARD

5. In a medium saucepan over medium-high heat, combine the heavy cream, milk, sugar, cocoa powder, vanilla, and salt. In a small bowl, whisk together the egg yolks and cornstarch. In a medium bowl, set aside the dark chocolate. Once the cream mixture starts to boil, pour a little into the egg-yolk mixture while whisking. Pour the egg-yolk mixture into the saucepan and whisk until the custard starts to thicken up. Remove from the heat and pour over the dark chocolate. Whisk until smooth. Pour the custard into the piecrust and refrigerate for at least 4 hours.

TO MAKE THE CHERRY JAM

6. In a medium saucepan over medium heat, combine the cherries, sugar, lemon juice, and pectin and cook until most of the water has evaporated and the mixture appears syrupy. Transfer to a food processor and pulse a few times until you get a chunky jam. Pour the jam over the chilled custard and smooth it out evenly with a spatula. Chill in the refrigerator for 1 hour.

7. In a stand mixer fitted with a whisk attachment, whip the chilled ganache and remaining ½ cup of heavy cream (113 grams) until stiff peaks form. Top the chilled pie with the whipped ganache and smooth it out with a spatula.

Fancy it up: Try dressing up your finished pie with chocolate shavings and maraschino cherries.

BANANA SPLIT ICE CREAM PIE WITH STRAWBERRY JAM AND MAGIC SHELL

Yield: 1 (9-inch) deep-dish pie **Total time:** 10 hours 45 minutes

In this recipe, I've turned a banana split with all the toppings into a delicious pie. A layer of flaky Cocoa Crust is the base for a creamy banana ice cream, homemade strawberry jam, dark chocolate magic shell, and chopped peanuts to top. The no-churn banana ice cream translated in pastry terms is a semifreddo. This means it never freezes all the way, so you can serve it right out of the freezer.

Equipment: Rolling pin, 9-inch deep-dish pie plate, parchment paper, pie weights, mixing bowls, measuring cups or kitchen scale, measuring spoons, saucepan, metal bowl, whisk, stand mixer with whisk attachment, spatula, microwave-safe bowl

FOR THE CRUST

Single batch Cocoa Crust (page 26)

FOR THE NO-CHURN BANANA ICE CREAM

½ cup mashed banana (from 1 small banana)

1 tablespoon freshly squeezed lemon juice (14 grams)

½ cup granulated sugar (100 grams)

3 egg whites

¾ cup heavy cream (170 grams)

1 teaspoon vanilla extract

¼ teaspoon salt

TO BLIND-BAKE THE CRUST

1. Prepare a batch of the Cocoa Crust.

2. Preheat the oven to 375°F. Unwrap the dough onto a lightly floured work surface. Lightly flour a rolling pin and begin rolling from the center outward. Roll the dough into a circle roughly 16 inches in diameter. Drape the dough over your rolling pin, then transfer to a deep-dish pie plate. Trim and crimp the edges. Freeze the piecrust for 10 minutes.

3. Remove the piecrust from the freezer. Lay a large piece of parchment paper over the center of the dish and fill with pie weights. Blind-bake in the preheated oven for 20 minutes. Remove the weights and bake for an additional 15 minutes. Cool completely at room temperature (about 15 minutes while you make the ice cream).

FOR THE STRAWBERRY JAM

1 (8-ounce) package
fresh or frozen
strawberries
(227 grams)

½ cup granulated
sugar (100 grams)

1 tablespoon freshly
squeezed lemon
juice (14 grams)

FOR THE MAGIC SHELL

¾ cup chocolate chips
(108 grams)

2 teaspoons
coconut oil

¼ cup chopped
peanuts (30 grams)

TO MAKE THE NO-CHURN BANANA ICE CREAM

4. In a medium bowl, sprinkle the mashed banana with the lemon juice. Prepare a double boiler by filling a saucepan with 2 cups of water and heat to a simmer. Place the sugar and egg whites in a metal bowl over the simmering water. Whisk until the sugar dissolves and the egg whites are warm to the touch. Transfer the mixture to a stand mixer fitted with a whisk attachment and whip until stiff peaks form. Set aside. In a large bowl, combine the heavy cream, vanilla, and salt and whip until stiff peaks form. Fold in the mashed banana and egg white mixture until smooth. Pour into the piecrust and smooth it out evenly with a spatula. Freeze for at least 8 hours or overnight.

TO MAKE THE STRAWBERRY JAM

5. In a small saucepan, combine the strawberries, sugar, and lemon juice. Cook over medium-high heat, stirring frequently, for 20 minutes, or until the strawberries have broken down and most of the water has evaporated. Pour the jam over the frozen banana ice cream and smooth out evenly with a spatula. Freeze for 1 hour.

continued >

TO MAKE THE MAGIC SHELL

6. In a microwave-safe bowl, combine the chocolate chips and coconut oil and heat in the microwave in 30-second increments until fully melted. Pour the chocolate over the frozen pie quickly and smooth it out with a spatula as fast as you can since the shell will harden rapidly. Immediately garnish with chopped peanuts. Freeze until ready to serve.

Oh no! If the chocolate magic shell sets up before you can sprinkle over the peanuts, use a blow-torch to melt the chocolate again, then try adding the peanuts.

Get ahead: This whole pie can be made several days in advance, or you can break up the steps by completing one stage each day until ready to serve.

TAHINI-HONEY PIE

Yield: 1 (9-inch) standard pie **Total time:** 2 hours 45 minutes

Tahini is made from toasted white sesame seeds. It's ground up similar to peanut butter and has a salty, nutty taste. I love this honey and tahini pairing because you might not be able to quite put your finger on the flavors, but you'll know you like it. Use a leaf-shaped cookie cutter to turn any dough scraps into decoration. Bake them separately for 10 minutes in the preheated oven while the crust chills and use them as garnish along with the sesame seeds.

Equipment: Rolling pin, 9-inch pie plate, sheet pan, parchment paper, pie weights, mixing bowl, measuring cups or kitchen scale, measuring spoons, whisk

Single batch Gluten-Free Crust (page 22), or All-Butter Crust (page 20) if not gluten-free

¾ cup honey (255 grams)

½ cup tahini (113 grams)

8 tablespoons melted unsalted butter (113 grams)

¼ cup brown sugar (50 grams)

3 eggs

1 tablespoon apple cider vinegar (14 grams)

2 teaspoons cornstarch

1½ teaspoons salt

1 teaspoon vanilla extract

1 tablespoon white sesame seeds

1. Prepare a batch of the Gluten-Free Crust or All-Butter Crust.

2. Preheat the oven to 375°F. Unwrap the dough onto a lightly floured work surface. Lightly flour a rolling pin and begin rolling from the center outward. Roll the dough into a circle roughly 16 inches in diameter. Drape the dough over your rolling pin, then transfer to a pie plate. Trim and crimp the edges, reserving any dough scraps for decoration (see headnote). Freeze the piecrust for 10 minutes.

3. Remove the piecrust from the freezer. Lay a large piece of parchment paper over the center of the dish and fill with pie weights. Blind-bake the crust in the preheated oven for 20 minutes.

4. In a large bowl, combine the honey, tahini, melted butter, brown sugar, eggs, apple cider vinegar, cornstarch, salt, and vanilla and whisk until smooth. Reduce the oven to 350°F. Pour the filling into the crust and bake for 35 minutes. Cool for 1 hour in the refrigerator.

5. Garnish the pie with white sesame seeds. Serve the pie chilled.

PUMPKIN BREAD CHEESECAKE WITH SPICED PEPITA STREUSEL

Yield: 1 (9-inch) cheesecake **Total time:** 10 hours 45 minutes

Plain pumpkin cheesecake is a thing of the past. Don't get me wrong; the flavors are great, but there are many ways to improve on the classic. This no-bake cheesecake uses pumpkin bread as the crust. Pumpkin puree keeps this creative "crust" extremely tender and moist. It's wonderful by itself, but it really comes to life when it's topped with a creamy cheesecake filling and a crunchy pepita streusel.

Equipment: Mixing bowls, measuring cups or kitchen scale, measuring spoons, sheet pan, parchment paper, 9-inch springform pan, whisk, stand mixer with paddle attachment, spatula

FOR THE SPICED PEPITA STREUSEL

¼ cup pepitas
(29 grams)

2 tablespoons melted unsalted butter
(28 grams)

2 tablespoons brown sugar (25 grams)

¼ teaspoon ground cinnamon

⅛ teaspoon ground allspice

⅛ teaspoon salt

TO MAKE THE SPICED PEPITA STREUSEL

1. Preheat the oven to 350°F. In a medium bowl, combine pepitas, melted butter, brown sugar, cinnamon, allspice, and salt and toss to coat. Pour the pepitas onto a sheet pan lined with parchment paper and bake for 10 minutes. Let cool at room temperature and store in an airtight container for later.

TO MAKE THE PUMPKIN BREAD

2. Spray a springform pan with nonstick baking spray. In a large bowl, combine the flour, pumpkin, sugar, oil, egg, baking powder, cinnamon, baking soda, ginger, and salt and mix well. Pour the batter into the springform pan. Bake for 20 minutes, or until a toothpick inserted in the middle comes out clean. Let the pumpkin bread cool at room temperature for 2 hours or in the refrigerator for 1 hour.

continued >

FOR THE PUMPKIN BREAD

Nonstick baking spray

1¼ cups flour (160 grams)

1 cup pumpkin puree
(226 grams)

½ cup granulated sugar
(100 grams)

⅓ cup canola oil (76 grams)

1 egg

1 teaspoon
baking powder

1 teaspoon
ground cinnamon

½ teaspoon baking soda

½ teaspoon
ground ginger

½ teaspoon salt

FOR THE CHEESECAKE FILLING

1 cup heavy cream
(226 grams)

½ teaspoon
vanilla extract

2 (8-ounce) packages
cream cheese,
room temperature
(454 grams)

½ cup granulated sugar
(100 grams)

TO MAKE THE CHEESECAKE FILLING

3. In a medium bowl, combine the heavy cream and vanilla and whip until stiff peaks form, then set aside. In a stand mixer fitted with a paddle attachment, mix the cream cheese and sugar until smooth, scraping down the sides as needed. Fold the whipped cream into the cream cheese mixture until smooth. Pour the filling into the pan on top of the banana bread and smooth it out with a spatula. Chill in the refrigerator for at least 8 hours or overnight.

4. Before serving, garnish with the spiced pepita streusel.

MILK CHOCOLATE, CARAMEL, AND HAZELNUT CRUNCH PIE

Yield: 1 (9-inch) deep-dish pie **Total time:** 8 hours

I almost called this pie "Candy Bar Pie" since it reminds me of a caramel-y, nutty candy bar. Milk chocolate custard is set over a flaky Cocoa Crust, then covered in a layer of salted caramel and topped with a crunchy hazelnut praline. This pie is absolutely decadent and all you can ask for in a dessert.

Equipment: Rolling pin, 9-inch deep-dish pie plate, parchment paper, pie weights, measuring cups or kitchen scale, sheet pan, silicone mat, mixing bowls, measuring spoons, saucepan, whisk, plastic wrap, spatula, large skillet (not nonstick), food processor

FOR THE CRUST

Single batch Cocoa Crust (page 26)

FOR THE HAZELNUT PRALINE

1 cup skinned hazelnuts (150 grams)

⅔ cup granulated sugar, divided (135 grams)

½ teaspoon salt

TO BLIND-BAKE THE CRUST

1. Prepare a batch of the Cocoa Crust.

2. Preheat the oven to 375°F. Unwrap the dough onto a lightly floured work surface. Lightly flour a rolling pin and begin rolling from the center outward. Roll the dough into a circle roughly 16 inches in diameter. Drape the dough over your rolling pin, then transfer to a deep-dish pie plate. Trim and crimp the edges. Freeze the piecrust for 10 minutes.

3. Remove the piecrust from the freezer. Lay a large piece of parchment paper over the center of the dish and fill with pie weights. Blind-bake in the preheated oven for 20 minutes. Remove the weights and bake for an additional 15 minutes. Cool completely at room temperature (about 15 minutes while you continue the recipe).

4. While the oven is on, toast the hazelnuts for the praline. On a sheet pan lined with a silicone mat, toast the hazelnuts for 5 to 8 minutes, watching carefully so they don't burn. Cool at room temperature and set aside until needed.

continued >

FOR THE MILK CHOCOLATE CUSTARD

1 cup milk chocolate, chopped (144 grams)

4 egg yolks

2 tablespoons cornstarch (15 grams)

1½ cups heavy cream (339 grams)

⅓ cup granulated sugar (68 grams)

¼ teaspoon salt

FOR THE CARAMEL

½ cup heavy cream (113 grams)

3 tablespoons unsalted butter (42 grams)

⅛ teaspoon salt

¾ cup granulated sugar (150 grams)

¼ cup water

TO MAKE THE MILK CHOCOLATE CUSTARD

5. In a large bowl, set aside the milk chocolate. In a small bowl, whisk the egg yolks and cornstarch together and set aside. In a medium saucepan over medium-high heat, combine the heavy cream, sugar, and salt. Once the mixture is hot, stream a little into the egg yolks while whisking. Pour the egg-yolk mixture into the saucepan and cook until thick, then immediately pour over the chocolate and whisk until smooth. Pour the custard into the cooled crust. Place a piece of plastic wrap over the surface of the custard and chill in the refrigerator for at least 4 hours.

TO MAKE THE CARAMEL

6. In a small saucepan over medium-high heat, combine the heavy cream, butter, and salt and heat until melted together. In a separate saucepan over medium-high heat, combine the sugar and water and heat until the sugar dissolves and the mixture appears amber in color. Do not stir during this time. Once the sugar has turned amber, remove from the heat and whisk in the cream mixture a little at a time. The sugar will bubble up, so be careful. Continue to whisk in the cream mixture until fully incorporated. Pour the caramel over the chilled custard and smooth it out with a spatula. Chill in the refrigerator for at least 2 hours.

7. In a large skillet (not a nonstick skillet), heat ⅓ cup of sugar (67.5 grams) over medium-high heat until the sugar begins to melt and caramelize. Do not stir, but swirl the pan if needed. Once the sugar has melted, sprinkle over the remaining ⅓ cup of sugar (67.5 grams). Reduce the heat to medium-low and swirl the pan to mix it. The caramel will eventually melt together. Once melted, pour the caramel over the hazelnuts and allow it to cool completely at room temperature for 30 to 45 minutes. Once cooled, break into pieces and place in a food processor. Process until it has all broken up. Add the salt and process again. Top the pie with the hazelnut praline and chill until ready to serve.

Don't have that? You can substitute pretty much any other nut of your choosing for the praline. Cashews, almonds, pistachios, and pecans are all great options.

More on that: If you can't find skinned hazelnuts, you can skin them yourself. Toast the hazelnuts in a preheated oven at 350°F for 10 minutes. Cool at room temperature for 5 minutes, then peel the skins off.

VANILLA BEAN BASQUE CHEESECAKE

Yield: 1 (9-inch) cheesecake **Total time:** 5 hours 15 minutes

Cheesecake is such a crowd-pleasing dessert, because it's creamy and silky smooth, and the balance of sweetness and tanginess is outstanding. If you like cheesecake, you must try baking up this one, which is shockingly easy to make. Basque cheesecake is a rustic, crustless cheesecake that is cooked on high heat, caramelizing the outside but keeping the center perfectly creamy.

Equipment: 9-inch springform pan, parchment paper, stand mixer with paddle attachment, measuring cups or kitchen scale, measuring spoons, spatula

Nonstick baking spray

4 (8-ounce) packages cream cheese, at room temperature (904 grams)

1½ cups granulated sugar (300 grams)

¼ cup flour (34 grams)

1 teaspoon vanilla paste or ½ vanilla bean pod

1 teaspoon salt

1¾ cups heavy cream (396 grams)

5 eggs

1. Preheat the oven to 400°F.

2. Lightly spray a springform pan with nonstick baking spray. Line the pan with parchment paper. Allow the parchment paper to cover the bottom and go all the way up the sides, higher than the edge of the pan. This cheesecake will rise over the top of the pan, then deflate once cooled.

3. In a stand mixer fitted with a paddle attachment, mix the cream cheese and sugar together. Combine until smooth, scraping down the sides as needed. Add the flour, vanilla, and salt and continue mixing. Add the heavy cream, a little at a time. Finally, add the eggs, one at a time, and continue mixing until fully combined. Pour the cheesecake filling into the prepared springform pan. Bake for 1 hour. Cheesecake will have risen high and should appear burnt on the top. It will not appear completely set, but this is okay.

4. Let the cheesecake cool at room temperature for just 1 hour to serve warm and creamy. To serve chilled and set, let the cheesecake chill in the refrigerator for at least 4 hours.

Fancy it up: This cheesecake is perfectly delicious on its own, but if you'd like to spruce it up, try serving with a mound of fresh berries in the center. Other serving options include fresh whipped cream, chocolate shavings, fruit jam, sliced bananas, or sliced tropical fruit.

WHITE RUSSIAN CREAM PIE WITH BROWN BUTTER GRAHAM CRUST

Yield: 1 (9-inch) deep-dish pie **Total time:** 8 hours 45 minutes

A few years ago, my then-fiancé and I went on a cruise in Italy. I stayed sober due to seasickness, but my husband tried the entire cocktail list, loving the White Russian the best. He drank many of them during that trip, and how can you blame him? It's basically a dessert in a drink. When we got back, we bought all the liquors to make it and added in RumChata, a cinnamon milk liquor. This pie tastes exactly like our beloved cocktail.

Equipment: Saucepan, measuring cups or kitchen scale, measuring spoons, food processor, 9-inch springform pan, blender, mixing bowl, whisk, plastic wrap, stand mixer with whisk attachment, spatula

---

FOR THE BROWN BUTTER GRAHAM CRUST

10 tablespoons unsalted butter (141 grams)

2 cups graham cracker crumbs, from 12 sheets of crackers (170 grams)

¼ cup brown sugar (50 grams)

¼ teaspoon salt

Nonstick baking spray

TO MAKE THE BROWN BUTTER GRAHAM CRUST

1. Preheat the oven to 350°F. In a small saucepan over medium-high heat, heat the butter until it has fully melted and the milk solids start to caramelize. The butter will start to turn foamy and smell nutty. Remove from the heat and set aside.

2. In a food processer, combine the graham cracker crumbs, brown sugar, and salt together and mix. Stream in the browned butter and mix to combine. Lightly spray a springform pan with nonstick baking spray. Pour the crumbs into the springform pan and press them down firmly in the bottom and up the sides to create the crust. Bake for 10 minutes, then let cool at room temperature.

FOR THE FILLING

½ cup white chocolate chips (70 grams)

1 tablespoon vodka (14 grams)

4 egg yolks

¼ cup cornstarch (30 grams)

1½ cups heavy cream (339 grams)

½ cup granulated sugar (100 grams)

¼ cup RumChata liqueur (56 grams)

2 tablespoons Irish cream liqueur (28 grams)

2 tablespoons Kahlúa liqueur (28 grams)

½ teaspoon salt

¼ teaspoon ground cinnamon

FOR THE WHIPPED CREAM

1 cup heavy cream (226 grams)

½ cup confectioners' sugar (60 grams)

½ teaspoon vanilla extract

TO MAKE THE FILLING

3. Place the white chocolate chips and vodka in a blender and set aside. In a small bowl, whisk the egg yolks and cornstarch to combine, then set aside. In a medium saucepan over medium-high heat, combine the heavy cream, sugar, RumChata, Irish cream, Kahlúa, salt, and cinnamon. Once the cream mixture is hot, stream a little into the egg-yolk mixture and whisk well. Pour the egg-yolk mixture into the saucepan and cook while whisking until the custard becomes very thick. Immediately pour the custard into the blender with the chocolate chips. Process until smooth and fully incorporated. Pour the custard into the piecrust, cover tightly with plastic wrap, and chill in the refrigerator for at least 8 hours or overnight.

TO MAKE THE WHIPPED CREAM

4. In a stand mixer fitted with a whisk attachment, whip the heavy cream, sugar, and vanilla until stiff peaks form. Top the pie with the whipped cream and smooth it out with a spatula.

Fancy it up: To create a modern design, smooth the whipped cream into an even layer over the top of the pie, then freeze it for 20 minutes. Place a decorative stencil over the chilled pie, sprinkle all over with cinnamon, and carefully remove the stencil to reveal the design.

BLACK SESAME FRANGIPANE PIE WITH DOUBLE CHOCOLATE GANACHE

Yield: 1 (9-inch) standard pie **Total time:** 2 hours 45 minutes

I'm very adventurous when it comes to food, and I love to experiment to see what different flavors enhance each other. Surprisingly, black sesame and dark chocolate play very well together, and I urge you to try out the combination in this pie. Black sesame is ground up and baked into a custard, then topped with a layer of standard chocolate ganache as well as a creamy whipped chocolate ganache. Whipped ganache is denser than a whipped cream and lighter than a mousse. Be sure to make it first so it has time to set overnight in order to whip properly.

Equipment: Microwave-safe bowls, measuring cups or kitchen scale, measuring spoons, plastic wrap, rolling pin, 9-inch pie plate, parchment paper, pie weights, food processor, spatula, stand mixer with whisk attachment

FOR THE MILK CHOCOLATE WHIPPED GANACHE

1½ cups heavy cream, divided (339 grams)

1 cup milk chocolate chips (144 grams)

FOR THE CRUST

Single batch Cocoa Crust (page 26)

TO MAKE THE MILK CHOCOLATE WHIPPED GANACHE

1. In a microwave-safe bowl, combine ¾ cup of heavy cream (169.5 grams) and the milk chocolate chips and microwave until melted. Cool the ganache in the refrigerator. Once cooled, cover with plastic wrap and chill overnight.

TO BLIND-BAKE THE CRUST

2. Prepare a batch of the Cocoa Crust.

3. Preheat the oven to 375°F. Unwrap the dough onto a lightly floured work surface. Lightly flour a rolling pin and begin rolling from the center outward. Roll the dough into a circle roughly 16 inches in diameter. Drape the dough over your rolling pin, then transfer to a pie plate. Trim and crimp the edges. Freeze the piecrust for 10 minutes.

FOR THE BLACK SESAME FRANGIPANE

1 cup black sesame seeds (142 grams)

8 tablespoons melted unsalted butter (113 grams)

¼ cup granulated sugar (50 grams)

2 eggs

2 tablespoons flour (16 grams)

½ teaspoon salt

FOR THE DARK CHOCOLATE GANACHE

¾ cup chocolate chips (108 grams)

½ cup heavy cream (113 grams)

4. Remove the piecrust from the freezer. Lay a large piece of parchment paper over the center of the dish and fill with pie weights. Blind-bake in a pre-heated oven for 20 minutes.

TO MAKE THE BLACK SESAME FRANGIPANE

5. In a food processor, blend the black sesame seeds to break them up. Add the butter, sugar, eggs, flour, and salt and blend until smooth. Pour into the blind-baked crust and bake for an additional 15 minutes. Cool in the refrigerator for 1 hour.

TO MAKE THE DARK CHOCOLATE GANACHE

6. In a microwave-safe bowl, combine the chocolate and heavy cream and microwave in 30-second increments until melted. Stir until combined. Pour the dark chocolate ganache over the cooled filling and smooth it out with a spatula. Chill for 1 hour.

7. In a stand mixer fitted with a whisk attachment, whip the cooled milk chocolate ganache and remaining ¾ cup of heavy cream (169.5 grams). Whip until stiff peaks form. Top the pie with the milk chocolate whipped ganache and smooth it out with a spatula.

Fancy it up: Try using a pastry bag fitted with a star piping tip to top the pie with the milk chocolate whipped ganache. Decorate with rosettes, stars, or a combination of both.

Beer Cheese Hand Pies, page 100

CHAPTER 5

Beyond the Pie Plate

Pies come in all shapes and forms. This chapter is all about creating free-form pies that don't need a pie plate at all. Handheld pies are great for a sweet treat or a savory appetizer, and slab pies are fantastic options to serve to a large crowd.

CHORIZO AND OAXACA CHEESE HAND PIES

Yield: 10 hand pies **Total time:** 1 hour 20 minutes

My husband goes nuts for chorizo, so naturally I wanted to make a hand pie that he'd love. And if you're a fan of queso fundido, this hand pie is also for you. Chorizo's super savory, spicy flavor goes perfectly with melty, gooey Oaxaca cheese. I've tucked it all inside a Cornmeal Crust to give it more of a taco-inspired flair. If you can't find Mexican chorizo, you can easily substitute dried chorizo.

Equipment: Sauté pan, measuring cups or kitchen scale, grater, rolling pin, 4-inch round cookie cutter, mixing bowl, whisk, measuring spoons, sheet pan, parchment paper, pastry brush, fork, knife

Single batch Cornmeal Crust (page 25)

8 ounces Mexican chorizo (227 grams)

4 ounces Oaxaca cheese (113 grams)

1 egg

2 tablespoons water

1. Prepare one batch of the Cornmeal Crust.

2. In a sauté pan over medium-high heat, fully cook the chorizo. Drain the fat and let the chorizo cool at room temperature.

3. Using a grater, shred the Oaxaca cheese and set it aside.

4. Preheat the oven to 425°F. Unwrap the dough onto a lightly floured work surface. Lightly flour a rolling pin and begin rolling from the center outward until ⅛ inch thick. Use a 4-inch round cookie cutter to cut out as many pieces as possible. Gather any dough scraps together and reroll to the same thickness to cut out more pieces.

5. In a small bowl, whisk together the egg and water to make an egg wash.

6. Line a sheet pan with parchment paper. Brush each circle of dough with the egg wash. Place 1 tablespoon of chorizo and 1 tablespoon of cheese inside the center of each circle, leaving ½ inch of dough clean around the perimeter. Bring the edges of the dough together, creating a half-moon shape. Seal the dough with a fork around the edges. Place sealed pies on the sheet pan about 1 inch apart. Continue to fill and seal each hand pie, then brush the top of each pie with egg wash. Chill in the freezer for 10 minutes.

7. Before baking, use a knife to poke 2 holes on top of each hand pie to vent. Bake for 18 minutes, or until pies are evenly golden brown. Cool at room temperature for 5 minutes, then serve immediately.

Fancy it up: Try serving this hand pie with a side of poblano pepper relish. Char 1 large poblano pepper over a high flame. Transfer to a bowl and cover with plastic wrap for 10 minutes, then peel off the poblano's skin and dice it into small pieces. Heat a sauté pan over high heat with 2 tablespoons of butter until melted, then add 2 cups of corn, the chopped poblano pepper, 1 teaspoon ground cumin, and salt and pepper to taste.

BEER CHEESE HAND PIES

Yield: 10 hand pies **Total time:** 1 hour 45 minutes

I scream, you scream, we all scream for *beer cheese*! Beer cheese is a delicious dip that I'd been longing to stuff into a hand pie. If you've ever had this dip before, you know just how irresistibly delicious it is. There is something about beer and cheese that makes you want to keep going back in for another bite. I personally like to use a lightly hopped wheat ale in this recipe, but feel free to use your favorite beer. Malted and hoppy beers are both great options.

Equipment: Saucepan, measuring cups or kitchen scale, measuring spoons, mixing bowls, plastic wrap, whisk, rolling pin, 4-inch round cookie cutter, sheet pan, parchment paper, pastry brush, fork, knife

---

Single batch
All-Butter Crust
(page 20)

4 tablespoons
unsalted butter
(57 grams)

¼ cup flour
(32 grams)

½ teaspoon
garlic powder

½ teaspoon
onion powder

⅛ teaspoon cayenne

½ cup milk
(110 grams)

½ cup beer
(110 grams)

1 teaspoon
stone-ground
mustard

1. Prepare a batch of the All-Butter Crust.

2. In a small saucepan over medium-high heat, melt the butter. Once melted, add the flour, garlic powder, onion powder, and cayenne. Add the milk, a little at a time, and stir to combine. Continue to add the milk slowly, then add the beer and mix well. Add the mustard, then fold in the cheddar and mozzarella and continue to heat until completely melted. Add the salt and pepper and stir. Transfer the beer cheese to a medium bowl, cover the surface of the cheese with plastic wrap, and chill in the refrigerator for 1 hour, or until completely cooled.

3. Preheat the oven to 425°F. In a small bowl, whisk together the egg and water to make an egg wash.

4. Unwrap the dough onto a lightly floured work surface. Lightly flour a rolling pin and begin rolling from the center outward until ⅛ inch thick. Use a 4-inch round cookie cutter to cut out as many pieces as possible. Gather any dough scraps together and reroll to the same thickness to cut out more pieces.

½ cup shredded sharp cheddar (4 ounces, 113 grams)

½ cup shredded mozzarella (4 ounces, 113 grams)

¼ teaspoon salt

⅛ teaspoon freshly ground black pepper

1 egg

2 tablespoons water

5. Line a sheet pan with parchment paper. Brush each circle of dough with egg wash. Place 1 tablespoon of chilled beer cheese inside the center of each circle, leaving ½ inch of dough clean around the perimeter. Bring the edges of the dough together, creating a half-moon shape. Seal the dough with a fork around the edges. Place sealed pies on the sheet pan about 1 inch apart. Continue to fill and seal each hand pie, then brush the top of each pie with the egg wash. Chill in the freezer for 10 minutes.

6. Before baking, use a knife to poke 2 holes on top of each hand pie to vent. Bake for 18 minutes, or until pies are evenly golden brown. Cool at room temperature for 5 minutes and serve immediately.

Fancy it up: Did someone say jalapeño beer cheese? Try sprucing up your pies with jalapeño. Just chop up 1 jalapeño and add it to your beer cheese when you are folding in the cheeses.

RAINBOW SPRINKLE BIRTHDAY CAKE HAND PIES

Yield: 14 hand pies **Total time:** 2 hours 20 minutes

The filling in this recipe is my interpretation of the ultimate birthday cake flavor: Funfetti. I love the playfulness of these hand pies, and let's be honest, anytime I can go wild with rainbow sprinkles is a good day.

Equipment: Mixing bowls, measuring spoons, whisk, microwave-safe bowl, measuring cups or kitchen scale, stand mixer with paddle attachment, spatula, piping bag, rolling pin, ruler, knife, sheet pan, parchment paper, pastry brush, fork, knife, spoon

FOR THE CRUST

Double batch Gluten-Free Crust (page 22), or All-Butter Crust (page 20) if not gluten-free

1 egg

2 tablespoons water

FOR THE FILLING

1 cup white chocolate chips (6 ounces, 170 grams)

2 (8-ounce) packages cream cheese at room temperature (452 grams)

¼ cup granulated sugar (50 grams)

4 egg yolks

1 teaspoon rainbow sprinkles

TO MAKE THE CRUST

1. Prepare a double batch of the Gluten-Free Crust or All-Butter Crust.

2. In a small bowl, whisk together the egg and water to make an egg wash. Set aside.

TO MAKE THE FILLING

3. In a microwave-safe bowl, microwave the white chocolate in 30-second increments until fully melted, stirring in between. In a stand mixer fitted with a paddle attachment, mix the cream cheese. Add the melted white chocolate and sugar and mix again, scraping down the sides as needed. Add the egg yolks and mix well. Fold in the sprinkles by hand and transfer to a piping bag.

4. Preheat the oven to 350°F. Unwrap the dough onto a lightly floured work surface. Lightly flour a rolling pin and begin rolling from the center outward until the dough is ⅛ inch thick. Use a ruler to cut 2-by-3-inch rectangles, as many as possible.

FOR THE FROSTING

1 cup confectioners'
  sugar (120 grams)

1 tablespoon milk
  (15 grams)

2 teaspoons corn
  syrup (41 grams)

Rainbow sprinkles,
  to garnish

5. On a sheet pan lined with parchment paper, place half the rectangles about 1 inch apart from each other. Brush the edges of each rectangle with egg wash. Pipe out roughly 2 tablespoons of filling inside each rectangle, leaving a ½-inch border around the sides. Cover each filled rectangle with a corresponding top rectangle and seal with a fork all around. Brush each hand pie with more egg wash and freeze for 10 minutes.

6. Use a knife to poke 2 holes on top of each hand pie to vent. Bake the hand pies for 24 minutes. Cool at room temperature.

TO MAKE THE FROSTING

7. In a medium bowl, whisk together the confectioners' sugar, milk, and corn syrup. Use a spoon to smooth a dollop of frosting over each cooled hand pie. Garnish with rainbow sprinkles and let the frosting set at room temperature for 1 hour before serving.

Fancy it up: If you want to spruce up the white frosting, try adding some food gel to it. Just add it in while you're mixing the frosting. You can even divide the frosting into separate bowls to make multiple colors to decorate the pies with.

ROASTED STRAWBERRY SLAB PIE WITH BALSAMIC DRIZZLE

Yield: 1 (15-by-18-inch) slab pie **Total time:** 2 hours 35 minutes

During my childhood in California, I really didn't appreciate all of the wonderful produce grown in the state. That all changed when my mom took me to a strawberry festival in Ojai. The vendors there were making everything you can think of with strawberries: beer, pizza, and, of course, pie. I fell in love with strawberries, and now that I live in Colorado, I wish I could just drive over to Ojai and attend that festival again. One day.

Equipment: Rolling pin, 15-by-18-inch jelly roll pan, mixing bowl, measuring cups or kitchen scale, measuring spoons

Double batch Cornmeal Crust (page 25)

2 pounds fresh or (thawed) frozen strawberries

¼ cup cornstarch (30 grams)

¼ cup brown sugar (50 grams)

2 tablespoons freshly squeezed lemon juice

¼ teaspoon freshly ground black pepper

2 tablespoons aged balsamic vinegar

1. Prepare a double batch of the Cornmeal Crust.

2. Unwrap the dough onto a lightly floured work surface. Lightly flour a rolling pin and begin rolling from the center outward. Roll the dough into a 16-by-19-inch rectangle. Drape the dough over your rolling pin, then transfer onto a jelly roll pan. Trim and crimp the edges. Freeze the pan for 10 minutes.

3. Preheat the oven to 400°F.

4. In a large bowl, combine the strawberries, cornstarch, brown sugar, lemon juice, and pepper. Toss until evenly coated. Pour the filling into the jelly roll pan and bake for 30 minutes, then broil on high for 2 minutes to char the strawberries. Remove from the oven and drizzle the balsamic vinegar over the top. Cool at room temperature for 1 hour before serving.

PLUM AND CHERRY SLAB PIE WITH THYME-INFUSED HONEY

Yield: 1 (15-by-18-inch) slab pie **Total time:** 3 hours 50 minutes

It's great when stone fruits start to become available, because it's the first sign of my favorite season: summer. Sometimes the most satisfying end to a meal is to just bite into a juicy ripe stone fruit, but if you want to go a step further, this pie is a fantastic alternative. I love the way thyme pairs with fruit, and I try to sneak that flavor in as much as I can. In this recipe, thyme is infused in honey, which then sweetens the fruit in the filling. The thyme in the whole wheat crust brings out the flavor that much more.

Equipment: Rolling pin, 15-by-18-inch jelly roll pan, saucepan, measuring cups or kitchen scale, measuring spoons, mixing bowls, whisk, pastry brush, knife, pastry wheel

---

4 batches Whole Wheat Crust with Thyme (page 24)

¼ cup honey (85 grams)

3 sprigs fresh thyme

1½ pounds fresh or (thawed) frozen sliced plums

1 pound fresh or (thawed) frozen pitted cherries

¼ cup granulated sugar (50 grams)

¼ cup cornstarch (30 grams)

⅛ teaspoon salt

1 egg

2 tablespoons water

1. Prepare 4 batches of the Whole Wheat Crust with Thyme. You may only be able to fit 2 batches at a time in your food processor. After processing, combine each double batch as 1 wrapped disk for a total of 2 double-size disks of dough.

2. Unwrap one double batch of the dough onto a lightly floured work surface. Lightly flour a rolling pin and begin rolling from the center outward. Roll the dough into a 16-by-19-inch rectangle. Drape the dough over your rolling pin, then transfer onto a jelly roll pan. Trim and crimp the edges. Refrigerate the pan until the filling is ready.

3. In a small saucepan, combine the honey and thyme. Heat over medium-high heat until the honey begins to boil, then remove from the heat and let the flavors infuse for 10 minutes. Remove the thyme sprigs and let the honey cool at room temperature.

4. In a large bowl, combine the plums, cherries, sugar, cornstarch, salt, and infused honey and toss until evenly coated. In a small bowl, whisk together the egg and water to make an egg wash. Pour the fruit filling into the prepared jelly roll pan. Brush the sides of the crust with egg wash.

5. Preheat the oven to 350°F. Unwrap the other double batch of the dough onto a lightly floured work surface. Lightly flour a rolling pin and begin rolling from the center outward. Roll the dough into a 16-by-19-inch rectangle. Use a knife or pastry wheel to cut 16 (1-inch) strips. Arrange 8 strips over the filled pie from top to bottom. Take every other strip and fold it from the bottom to the top. Lay another strip down horizontally toward the top of the pie, then fold the strips back down. Continue to do this, alternating strips each time, until you have a lattice of 8 vertical strips and 8 horizontal ones. Trim the edges to hang ½ inch over the pan. Roll the overhanging dough to form a crust around the edge of the pan, then brush the remaining egg wash over the entire pie. Freeze the pie for 10 minutes before baking.

6. Bake the slab pie for 1 hour. Cool at room temperature for 1 hour before serving.

More on that: Frozen fruit is a great way to get these delicious flavors during an off-season. If you can't find frozen plums, frozen peaches make a perfect substitution. Just make sure to thaw the fruit before using in the filling.

APPLE AND PUMPKIN SLAB PIE WITH PECAN STREUSEL

Yield: 1 (15-by-18-inch) slab pie **Total time:** 3 hours 10 minutes

When Thanksgiving rolls around and you can't decide whether to bake an apple pie, pumpkin pie, or pecan pie, try this one out for size. This pie weaves together apple butter and a spiced pumpkin filling and is topped with a pecan and brown sugar streusel to bring all the flavors together. This is also the perfect option when you're trying to feed a crowd of Thanksgiving guests.

Equipment: Rolling pin, 15-by-18-inch jelly roll pan, knife, saucepan, measuring cups or kitchen scale, measuring spoons, blender, piping bag, mixing bowls, whisk, food processor, spatula, toothpick

FOR THE CRUST

Double batch
 All-Butter Crust
 (page 20)

FOR THE APPLE BUTTER

1 pound red apples

1 cup water

¼ cup apple cider
 vinegar (57 grams)

¼ cup granulated
 sugar (50 grams)

½ teaspoon
 ground cinnamon

¼ teaspoon salt

TO MAKE THE CRUST

1. Prepare a double batch of the All-Butter Crust.

2. Unwrap the dough onto a lightly floured work surface. Lightly flour a rolling pin and begin rolling from the center outward. Roll the dough into a 16-by-19-inch rectangle. Drape the dough over your rolling pin, then transfer onto a jelly roll pan. Trim and crimp the edges. Refrigerate the pan until the filling is ready.

TO MAKE THE APPLE BUTTER

3. Quarter and core the apples. In a small saucepan over medium-high heat, combine the apples with the water, apple cider vinegar, sugar, cinnamon, and salt. Cook for 30 minutes, or until most of the liquid has evaporated and the apples are cooked through. Transfer to a blender and blend until very smooth. Let the apple butter cool at room temperature while preparing the rest of the filling. Once cooled, transfer to a piping bag.

FOR THE PUMPKIN FILLING

1 (15-ounce) can
    pumpkin puree
    (425 grams)

1 cup milk (245 grams)

½ cup brown sugar
    (100 grams)

¼ cup granulated
    sugar (50 grams)

3 eggs

½ teaspoon salt

½ teaspoon
    ground cinnamon

½ teaspoon
    ground ginger

¼ teaspoon
    ground allspice

¼ teaspoon
    ground cloves

FOR THE PECAN STREUSEL

½ cup whole pecans
    (62 grams)

¼ cup flour (32 grams)

¼ cup oats (25 grams)

¼ cup brown sugar
    (50 grams)

4 tablespoons cold
    unsalted butter
    (57 grams)

¼ teaspoon salt

TO MAKE THE PUMPKIN FILLING

4. In a large bowl, combine the pumpkin, milk, brown sugar, granulated sugar, eggs, salt, cinnamon, ginger, allspice, and cloves and whisk until smooth. Set aside.

TO MAKE THE PECAN STREUSEL

5. In a food processor, mix the pecans, flour, oats, sugar, butter, and salt until the butter is incorporated. Transfer to a medium bowl and chill in the refrigerator until needed.

6. Preheat the oven to 350°F.

7. To fill the slab pie, pour the pumpkin filling into the crust first. Smooth it out to all the edges using a spatula. Pipe in stripes of apple butter and use a toothpick to weave the apple butter into the pumpkin. Sprinkle the streusel evenly over the top.

8. Bake the slab pie for 45 minutes. Cool at room temperature for 2 hours or in the refrigerator for 1 hour before serving.

> **Get ahead:** The apple butter can be made up to two weeks in advance. This will save 30 to 40 minutes off your total time. Just make as directed and save in an airtight container in the refrigerator until ready to use.

RASPBERRY HAND PIES WITH PISTACHIO FRANGIPANE

Yield: 14 hand pies **Total time:** 2 hours 30 minutes

When dreaming up new pairings for recipes, I try to think of all aspects of a dish. The ideal dessert features complementary flavors and contrasting textural components, and of course, it must be visually appealing. This recipe combines the sweet and sour flavor of raspberry with the salty, nutty crunch of pistachio. The end result is a stunning pink and green hand pie that's sure to impress.

Equipment: Mixing bowls, measuring spoons, whisk, blender, measuring cups or kitchen scale, fine-mesh strainer, saucepan, piping bags, food processor, rolling pin, ruler, knife, sheet pan, parchment paper, pastry brush

FOR THE CRUST

Double batch
   All-Butter Crust
   (page 20)

2 eggs

4 tablespoons water

FOR THE SEEDLESS RASPBERRY JAM

3 cups fresh
   raspberries
   (12 ounces,
   340 grams)

2 tablespoons freshly
   squeezed lemon
   juice (28 grams)

¼ cup granulated
   sugar (50 grams)

1 teaspoon pectin

TO MAKE THE CRUST

1. Prepare a double batch of the All-Butter Crust.

2. In a small bowl, whisk together the eggs and water to make an egg wash. Set aside.

TO MAKE THE SEEDLESS RASPBERRY JAM

3. In a blender, puree the raspberries and lemon juice. Strain the puree into a medium saucepan and discard the seeds. In a small bowl, whisk the sugar and pectin, then pour the mixture into the raspberry puree and mix well. Heat the saucepan on high and cook while stirring for 5 to 8 minutes, or until thick. Transfer the jam to a small bowl and let it cool at room temperature. Once cooled, transfer it to a piping bag, reserving 1 teaspoon of jam in the bowl to make the frosting later.

FOR THE PISTACHIO FRANGIPANE

1 cup toasted
pistachios
(113 grams)

¼ cup granulated
sugar (50 grams)

4 tablespoons melted
unsalted butter
(57 grams)

2 egg yolks

1 tablespoon flour
(9 grams)

¼ teaspoon salt

FOR THE RASPBERRY FROSTING

1 cup confectioners'
sugar (120 grams)

1 tablespoon milk
(15 grams)

2 teaspoons
corn syrup

1 teaspoon seedless
raspberry jam

2 tablespoons
chopped pistachios
to garnish

4. In a food processor, mix the pistachios, sugar, melted butter, egg yolks, flour, and salt until smooth. The pistachios will break down into uneven pieces, and that is okay. Transfer the frangipane to a piping bag and set aside.

5. Preheat the oven to 350°F.

6. Unwrap the dough onto a lightly floured work surface. Lightly flour a rolling pin and begin rolling from the center outward until the dough is ⅛ inch thick. Use a ruler to cut 2-by-3-inch rectangles, as many as possible. Place half of the rectangles on a sheet pan lined with parchment paper, about 1 inch apart from each other. Brush each rectangle with the egg wash. Pipe 2 lines of pistachio frangipane inside each rectangle lengthwise, leaving a ½-inch border around the sides and an empty space in the center. Pipe one line of raspberry jam in the center between the 2 lines of pistachio. Cover each pastry with a corresponding top piece of pie dough and seal with a fork all around. Brush each hand pie with more egg wash and freeze for 10 minutes.

7. Use a knife to poke 2 holes on top of each pie to vent. Bake the hand pies for 24 minutes. Cool at room temperature.

continued >

TO MAKE THE RASPBERRY FROSTING

8. In a small bowl, whisk together the confectioners' sugar, milk, corn syrup, and raspberry jam. Use a spoon to smooth it over each cooled hand pie. Garnish with chopped pistachios and let the frosting set at room temperature for 1 hour.

More on that: Raspberry pairs well with pretty much any nut of your choosing. You can substitute any other nut for a great new flavor combination, and I recommend trying cashews, almonds, or hazelnuts.

CRANBERRY, BRIE, WALNUT, AND HONEY HAND PIES

Yield: 12 hand pies **Total time:** 1 hour 25 minutes

Whenever there's a cheese board in sight, I immediately make a beeline for it. I can't help it; I'm all about every kind of cheese. These hand pies are a nod to one of my favorite party foods: the baked wheel of Brie cheese. I love how it's often paired with some kind of sweet jam and nuts, hitting all those wonderful flavors you're looking for in an appetizer. I've laid out an easy cranberry jam recipe for this hand pie, but if you have some leftover cranberry sauce from Thanksgiving, that will work just as well.

Equipment: Saucepan, measuring cups or kitchen scale, measuring spoons, mixing bowl, whisk, rolling pin, 3-inch round cookie cutter, sheet pan, parchment paper, pastry brush, fork, knife

---

Double batch Whole Wheat Crust with Thyme (page 24)

¾ cup fresh cranberries (75 grams)

¼ cup granulated sugar (50 grams)

¼ cup freshly squeezed orange juice (56 grams)

4 tablespoons water, divided

½ cup toasted walnuts (50 grams)

4 ounces Brie (113 grams)

1 egg

2 to 4 tablespoons honey (42 to 85 grams)

1. Prepare a double batch of the Whole Wheat Crust with Thyme.

2. In a small saucepan, combine the cranberries, sugar, orange juice, and 2 tablespoons of water and cook over medium heat for 10 to 15 minutes, or until the cranberries have broken down and the jam appears thick. Let the cranberry jam cool completely at room temperature.

3. Chop the toasted walnuts and set aside. Cut the Brie into small pieces and set aside. In a small bowl, whisk together the egg and the remaining 2 tablespoons of water to make an egg wash.

4. Preheat the oven to 425°F. Unwrap the dough onto a lightly floured work surface. Lightly flour a rolling pin and begin rolling from the center outward until the dough is ⅛ inch thick. Use a 3-inch round cookie cutter to cut circles out of the dough, as many as possible. Reroll the dough as needed. This recipe should yield 24 (3-inch) circles.

continued >

5. On a sheet pan lined with parchment paper, place half the circles about 1 inch apart from each other. Brush the perimeter of each circle with egg wash. Fill each circle with a few pieces of Brie, followed by 2 teaspoons of the cranberry jam, a sprinkle of the chopped walnuts, and a small drizzle of the honey. Leave a ½-inch border around the perimeter. Cover each filled circle with a corresponding top circle and seal with a fork all around. Brush the top of each hand pie with more egg wash and freeze for 10 minutes.

6. Before baking, use a knife to poke 2 holes on top of each hand pie to vent. Bake for 18 minutes, or until the hand pies are evenly golden brown. Cool at room temperature for 5 minutes and serve immediately.

Don't have that? During the off-season, it's hard to find fresh cranberries. Feel free to swap in raspberries instead. They are more commonly found throughout the year, and you can make your own jam or use store-bought for this recipe. If you want to make homemade jam, try my seedless raspberry jam in the recipe for Raspberry Hand Pies with Pistachio Frangipane (page 110).

Asparagus, Spinach, and Parmesan Galette with Sunny-Side-Up Egg, page 124

CHAPTER 6

Savory

Pie makes for a delicious dessert, but it also has a heartier savory side. In this chapter, you'll find a new spin on potpies and a few modern galettes. I'm a big fan of vegetables, so I've used a lot of them in here in different ways, along with a couple of meatier options.

PIZZA QUICHE WITH PEPPERONI, MOZZARELLA, AND JALAPEÑOS

Yield: 1 (9-inch) standard pie **Total time:** 2 hours 15 minutes

There are endless flavor combinations you can put in a quiche, but I thought I'd put an interesting spin on one with the pizza quiche. I've included some classic pizza ingredients inside, but you can get as creative as you like and add your favorites.

Equipment: Rolling pin, 9-inch pie plate, mixing bowl, measuring cups or kitchen scale, measuring spoons, whisk, parchment paper, pie weights

Single batch Gluten-Free Crust (page 22), or All-Butter Crust (page 20) if not gluten-free

¾ cup heavy cream (170 grams)

¾ cup milk (180 grams)

5 eggs

¾ teaspoon salt

¼ teaspoon freshly ground black pepper

1 cup shredded mozzarella (100 grams)

1 tablespoon diced jalapeño

2 ounces sliced pepperoni (57 grams)

1. Prepare a batch of the Gluten-Free Crust or All-Butter Crust.

2. Preheat the oven to 375°F. Unwrap the dough onto a lightly floured work surface. Lightly flour a rolling pin and begin rolling from the center outward. Roll the dough into a circle roughly 16 inches in diameter. Drape the dough over your rolling pin, then transfer to a pie plate. Trim and crimp the edges. Freeze the piecrust for 10 minutes while preparing the filling.

3. In a large bowl, combine the heavy cream, milk, eggs, salt, and pepper and whisk well. Fold in the mozzarella and jalapeño and set aside.

4. Remove the piecrust from the freezer. Lay a large piece of parchment paper over the center of the dish and fill with pie weights. Blind-bake in the preheated oven for 20 minutes. Remove the pie weights, pour in the filling, and top with sliced pepperoni. Return the pie to the oven, reduce the heat to 350°F, and bake for 45 minutes.

5. Let the pie cool at room temperature for 20 to 30 minutes before serving.

Don't have that? The pepperoni in this recipe can be interchanged with any cured meat of your choosing. Salami, chorizo, or even breakfast sausage are great substitutes. Just make sure the meat you're using is already cooked through, or precook it before adding it to the quiche.

CARAMELIZED SHALLOT TARTE TATIN WITH ARUGULA SALAD

Yield: 1 (10-inch) tarte tatin **Total time:** 1 hour 40 minutes

Shallots have a subtle sweet flavor, and I use them whenever possible. This pie is a particularly fun showcase for shallots, because it's baked upside down. First, you'll roast the shallots, then make a caramel with balsamic vinegar and sugar. After coating the shallots in the caramel, you'll top them with pie dough and bake it all together. The dish is then inverted onto a serving dish and topped with a fresh arugula salad to cut some of the richness. It may seem daunting, but this pie is well worth the effort.

Equipment: Mixing bowls, measuring cups or kitchen scale, measuring spoons, sheet pan, aluminum foil, cast-iron skillet, rolling pin

---

Single batch Whole Wheat Crust with Thyme (page 24)

6 large shallots, peeled and halved lengthwise (1 pound)

2 tablespoons olive oil (28 grams)

½ teaspoon salt

¼ cup balsamic vinegar (60 grams)

1 teaspoon granulated sugar

1 teaspoon unsalted butter

1 teaspoon fresh thyme

2 cups arugula (40 grams)

1 tablespoon freshly squeezed lemon juice (14 grams)

1. Prepare a batch of the Whole Wheat Crust with Thyme.

2. Preheat the oven to 400°F. In a medium bowl, toss the shallots with the olive oil and salt. Place on a sheet pan lined with aluminum foil and roast for 20 minutes.

3. In a cast-iron skillet over medium-high heat, combine the balsamic vinegar and sugar. Reduce for 5 minutes, or until slightly thick and syrupy. Remove from the heat and stir in the butter. Arrange the roasted shallots in the skillet in an even layer over the reduced balsamic vinegar, cut-side up.

4. Unwrap the dough onto a lightly floured work surface. Lightly flour a rolling pin and begin rolling from the center outward. Roll the dough into a circle roughly 16 inches in diameter. Drape the dough over your rolling pin, then transfer to the skillet, laying the dough over the shallots. Trim the sides or tuck them into the skillet.

5. Bake for 20 minutes. Let cool at room temperature for 5 minutes, then carefully invert onto a serving dish. Sprinkle with the fresh thyme.

6. In a medium bowl, mix the arugula and lemon juice, then spread the arugula over the pie. Serve immediately.

More on that: Shallots are easier to peel when you cut them in half first. Make sure you cut lengthwise, for the purposes of this recipe.

BUTTERNUT SQUASH, SPINACH, AND FETA GALETTE

Yield: 1 (9-inch) galette **Total time:** 2 hours 5 minutes

I am a huge fan of vegetables. I love them all, and I wanted to showcase some different flavor combinations in this savory vegetarian galette. For this recipe, I was inspired by Mediterranean cuisine. When roasted, butternut squash gets sweeter and is a great complement to hearty spinach and salty feta. The Cornmeal Crust adds another level of flavor for an unexpected twist.

Equipment: Mixing bowls, measuring cups or kitchen scale, measuring spoons, sheet pans, aluminum foil, large saucepan, fine-mesh strainer, large skillet, rolling pin, parchment paper, whisk, pastry brush

---

Single batch Cornmeal Crust (page 25)

4 cups diced butternut squash (from 1 medium squash)

3 tablespoons olive oil, divided (42 grams)

2 teaspoons salt, divided

Nonstick baking spray

1 (10-ounce) bag fresh spinach (284 grams)

2 cups sliced onions (from 1 small onion)

½ cup crumbled feta (37 grams)

1 egg

2 tablespoons water

1. Prepare a batch of the Cornmeal Crust.

2. Preheat the oven to 375°F. In a medium bowl, combine the butternut squash, 2 tablespoons of olive oil (28 grams), and 1 teaspoon of salt and toss to coat. Line a sheet pan with aluminum foil and spray with nonstick baking spray. Lay the butternut squash on the pan in an even layer. Roast for 30 minutes, or until tender.

3. In a large saucepan, combine the spinach and ½ teaspoon of salt over medium-high heat. Toss until fully cooked. Transfer the cooked spinach to a medium bowl and chill in the refrigerator. Once cooled, wring out any excess water by pressing the spinach against a fine-mesh strainer. Set aside.

4. In a large skillet, combine the onion slices, remaining 1 tablespoon of olive oil (14 grams), and remaining ½ teaspoon of salt and cook over medium-high heat. Stir continuously and cook until onions are translucent. Transfer to a medium bowl and set aside.

5. Unwrap the dough onto a lightly floured work surface. Lightly flour a rolling pin and begin rolling from the center outward. Roll the dough into a circle roughly 16 inches in diameter. Drape the dough over your rolling pin, then transfer to a sheet pan lined with parchment paper.

6. Fill the circle of dough with the spinach, onions, and butternut squash, leaving 2 inches around the edges. Top with the crumbled feta. Fold the edges of the dough in, on top of the filling.

7. In a small bowl, whisk together the egg and water to make an egg wash. Use a pastry brush to brush the egg wash over the dough. Freeze the pie for 10 minutes before baking. Bake for 35 minutes. Let cool at room temperature for 10 minutes before serving.

Get ahead: The butternut squash, spinach, and onions can be cooked several days in advance and stored in the refrigerator until ready to use.

ASPARAGUS, SPINACH, AND PARMESAN GALETTE WITH SUNNY-SIDE-UP EGG

Yield: 1 (12-inch) galette **Total time:** 1 hour 25 minutes

Raise your hand if you're always up for brunch. Sundays are for brunching with friends, and this galette would make the perfect addition to your spread. It's easy and fast to whip up, and you can do a lot of the work ahead of time. Make the dough and cook the asparagus and spinach the day before, then store in your refrigerator. When you're ready for brunch, just construct the galette and bake.

Equipment: Large saucepan, measuring cups or kitchen scale, measuring spoons, mixing bowls, fine-mesh strainer, large skillet, rolling pin, sheet pan, parchment paper, spoon, whisk, pastry brush

Single batch Whole Wheat Crust with Thyme (page 24)

1 (10-ounce) bag fresh spinach (284 grams)

1 teaspoon salt, divided

1 tablespoon olive oil (14 grams)

3 cups chopped asparagus (from 1 bunch)

1 teaspoon minced garlic

½ cup shredded Parmesan (50 grams)

2 eggs, divided

2 tablespoons water

1. Prepare a batch of the Whole Wheat Crust with Thyme.

2. In a large saucepan over medium-high heat, cook the spinach with ½ teaspoon of salt. Toss until fully cooked, then transfer the cooked spinach to a medium bowl and chill in the refrigerator. Once cooled, wring out any excess water by pressing the spinach against a fine-mesh strainer. Set aside.

3. In a large skillet over medium-high heat, heat the olive oil. Add the asparagus, garlic, and remaining ½ teaspoon of salt and cook for 5 minutes, or until the asparagus is tender. Transfer to a medium bowl and set aside.

4. Unwrap the dough onto a lightly floured work surface. Lightly flour a rolling pin and begin rolling from the center outward. Roll the dough into a circle roughly 16 inches in diameter. Drape the dough over your rolling pin, then transfer to a sheet pan lined with parchment paper.

5. Fill the center of the circle with the spinach and asparagus, leaving 2 inches around the edges. Top with the shredded Parmesan. Fold the edges of the dough in, on top of the filling. Use a spoon to make an indentation in the center where the egg will go.

6. Preheat the oven to 375°F. In a small bowl, whisk together 1 egg and the water to make an egg wash. Use a pastry brush to brush the egg wash over the dough. Freeze for 10 minutes before baking.

7. Crack the remaining egg into the indentation. Bake for 20 to 25 minutes, or until the whites have completely cooked. Serve immediately.

Fancy it up: Bacon would be a great addition to this galette. Dice 4 strips of bacon and render it off. Add the bacon to the spinach mixture before layering the fillings in the galette.

SWISS CHARD, CARAMELIZED ONION, AND ROASTED GARLIC GALETTE

Yield: 1 (12-inch) galette **Total time:** 2 hours 50 minutes

There's nothing like roasting garlic and caramelizing onions to get your kitchen smelling amazing. This galette is a great option for brunch, lunch, an appetizer, or even leftovers. It's layered with flavor-packed vegetables and makes a stunning dish.

Equipment: Knife, measuring spoons, aluminum foil, large skillet, measuring cups or kitchen scale, mixing bowls, mandoline, rolling pin, sheet pan, parchment paper, whisk, pastry brush

Single batch
Gluten-Free Crust
(page 22), or
All-Butter Crust
(page 20) if
not gluten-free

1 head of garlic

4 tablespoons
olive oil, divided
(60 grams)

4 tablespoons
unsalted butter
(57 grams)

2 pounds onions,
sliced (from
4 small onions)

1 tablespoon
granulated sugar
(13 grams)

2 teaspoons
salt, divided

1. Prepare a batch of the Gluten-Free Crust or All-Butter Crust.

2. Preheat the oven to 400°F. Cut the top off the head of garlic, then pour 1 tablespoon of olive oil (15 grams) over it and wrap in aluminum foil. Roast the garlic for 40 minutes, or until it looks dark and tender. Let it cool at room temperature.

3. In a large skillet over high heat, melt the butter. Add the onions, sugar, and 1 teaspoon of salt. Cook for 10 minutes, or until the onions are translucent. Add the vinegar, then reduce heat to low and continue cooking for about 45 minutes, stirring every 10 minutes or so. Transfer the onions to a small bowl and refrigerate for about 30 minutes.

4. In a large skillet over high heat, toss the Swiss chard with 1 tablespoon of olive oil (15 grams) and ½ teaspoon of salt. Cook until tender. Transfer to a small bowl and set aside.

5. With a mandoline, slice the red potatoes ⅛ inch thick. If you don't have a mandoline, cut the potatoes as thin as possible with a knife. In a large bowl, toss the sliced red potatoes with the remaining

¼ cup white wine vinegar (57 grams)

4 cups chopped Swiss chard (from 1 bunch)

2 red potatoes

½ cup shredded Asiago

1 egg

2 tablespoons water

2 tablespoons of olive oil (30 grams) and remaining ½ teaspoon of salt.

6. Unwrap the dough onto a lightly floured work surface. Lightly flour a rolling pin and begin rolling from the center outward. Roll the dough into a circle roughly 16 inches in diameter. Drape the dough over your rolling pin, then transfer to a sheet pan lined with parchment paper. In the skillet, combine the Swiss chard, caramelized onions, and roasted garlic and mix. Top the dough with the mixture, then sprinkle with the Asiago cheese, leaving 2 inches around the border clean. Lay the sliced red potatoes on top, overlapping one another by ¼ inch to cover the entire surface of the filling. Fold the edges of the dough in, on top of the potatoes.

7. Preheat the oven to 375°F. In a small bowl, whisk together the egg and water to make an egg wash. Use a pastry brush to brush the egg wash over the dough. Freeze the pie for 10 minutes.

8. Bake the galette for 40 minutes. Let it cool at room temperature for 5 minutes and serve.

Get ahead: The roasted garlic, caramelized onions, and Swiss chard can all be cooked up to a week in advance to help save time. Just keep them in a sealed container in the refrigerator until ready to use.

BUFFALO CHICKEN POTPIE WITH BLUE CHEESE

Yield: 1 (9-inch) standard pie **Total time:** 3 hours 10 minutes

If you're a fan of Buffalo chicken wings, this potpie is for you. It's not too spicy, stuffed with all the good stuff, and sprinkled with blue cheese crumbles before being topped with the second crust. Serve it with an ice-cold beer.

Equipment: Saucepan, measuring cups or kitchen scale, measuring spoons, mixing bowls, whisk, rolling pin, 9-inch pie plate, pastry brush, knife

---

Double batch
All-Butter Crust
(page 20)

4 tablespoons
unsalted butter
(57 grams)

1 cup diced onion
(from 1 small onion)
(52 grams)

1 cup diced celery
(from 2 stalks), plus
more sliced celery
stalks for serving
(101 grams)

1 cup diced carrot
(from 2 small
carrots), plus more
sliced carrots for
serving (57 grams)

1 tablespoon minced
garlic (8 grams)

1 teaspoon salt

½ teaspoon freshly
ground black pepper

1. Prepare a double batch of the All-Butter Crust.

2. In a large saucepan over medium-high heat, heat the butter until melted. Add the onion, celery, carrots, garlic, salt, pepper, and cayenne. Cook for 5 to 10 minutes, or until the onions are translucent. Add the cooked chicken, then sprinkle in the flour and toss to coat everything. In a medium bowl, mix together the chicken stock and Buffalo sauce, then add to the saucepan a little at a time, stirring frequently. Cook for 3 more minutes. Transfer the mixture to a large bowl and chill, uncovered, in the refrigerator for 1 hour. Cover with plastic wrap after 1 hour if you'll be refrigerating it for any longer.

3. In a small bowl, whisk together the egg and water to make an egg wash. Set aside.

4. Preheat the oven to 350°F. Unwrap one batch of the dough onto a lightly floured work surface. Lightly flour a rolling pin and begin rolling from the center outward. Roll the dough into a circle roughly 16 inches in diameter. Drape the dough over your rolling pin, then transfer to a pie plate. Let the edges hang over the dish for now. Pour the filling into the crust, then top with the blue cheese crumbles. Use a pastry brush to brush egg wash around the edges.

⅛ teaspoon cayenne

4 cups shredded
cooked chicken
(2 pounds
chicken thighs)

¼ cup flour
(34 grams)

¾ cup chicken stock
(180 grams)

½ cup Buffalo sauce
(120 grams)

1 egg

2 tablespoons water

¼ cup blue cheese
crumbles (37 grams)

Ranch dressing
for serving

5. Unwrap the other batch of the dough onto a lightly floured work surface. Lightly flour a rolling pin and begin rolling from the center outward. Roll the dough into a circle roughly 16 inches in diameter. Drape the dough over your rolling pin, then transfer to the top of the pie. Trim and crimp the edges together. Brush egg wash over the entire surface of the pie. Freeze the pie for 10 minutes.

6. Use a knife to cut an *X* at the top of the pie. Cut 4 more slits around the pie to vent. Bake the pie for 1 hour 30 minutes. Let cool at room temperature for 30 minutes before serving.

7. Serve the pie with additional blue cheese or with ranch dressing along with sliced carrots and celery.

Don't have that? If blue cheese isn't your thing, just leave it out. You can drizzle a little ranch dressing over each slice of pie instead.

MUSHROOM, LEEK, AND KALE POTPIE

Yield: 1 (9-inch) standard pie **Total time:** 3 hours 10 minutes

Mushrooms, leeks, and kale, oh my! If you're a vegetable fan like me, you'll love this potpie. This recipe calls for not one, not two, but three types of mushrooms cooked with some fresh kale and leeks. With all the levels of savory veggie flavor, you won't miss meat with this pie.

Equipment: Saucepan, measuring spoons, measuring cups or kitchen scale, mixing bowls, whisk, rolling pin, 9-inch pie plate, pastry brush, knife

Double batch
All-Butter Crust
(page 20)

2 tablespoons olive oil
(28 grams)

2 tablespoons
unsalted butter
(28 grams)

4 cups chopped kale
(from 1 bunch kale)

2 cups chopped leek
(from 1 large leek)

2 teaspoons
minced garlic

1½ teaspoons salt

8 ounces sliced
white mushrooms
(227 grams)

8 ounces sliced
crimini mushrooms
(227 grams)

1. Prepare a double batch of the All-Butter Crust.

2. In a large saucepan over medium-high heat, heat the olive oil and butter together. Add the kale, leek, garlic, and salt. Cook for about 5 minutes, or until the leek is translucent and the mixture has reduced in size. Add the white mushrooms, crimini mushrooms, and shiitake mushrooms and continue to cook until the mushrooms are tender. Add the flour and stir to coat. Add the broth a little at a time while stirring and cook for 3 more minutes. Transfer the mixture to a large bowl and chill in the refrigerator for about 1 hour.

3. In a small bowl, whisk together the egg and water to make an egg wash. Set aside.

4. Preheat the oven to 350°F. Unwrap one batch of the dough onto a lightly floured work surface. Lightly flour a rolling pin and begin rolling from the center outward. Roll the dough into a circle roughly 16 inches in diameter. Drape the dough over your rolling pin, then transfer to a pie plate. Leave the edges hanging over the dish for now. Pour the filling into the crust. Use a pastry brush to brush egg wash around the edges of the dough.

8 ounces sliced
shiitake mushrooms
(227 grams)

¼ cup flour
(34 grams)

1 cup vegetable broth
(226 grams)

1 egg

2 tablespoons water

5. Unwrap the other batch of the dough onto a lightly floured work surface. Lightly flour a rolling pin and begin rolling from the center outward. Roll the dough into a circle roughly 16 inches in diameter. Drape the dough over your rolling pin, then transfer to the top of the filled pie. Trim and crimp the edges together. Apply the remaining egg wash over the entire surface of the pie. Freeze the pie for 10 minutes.

6. Use a knife to cut an *X* at the top of the pie. Cut 4 more slits around the pie to vent. Bake the pie for 1 hour 30 minutes. Let it cool at room temperature for 30 minutes before serving.

More on that: When buying mushrooms, I choose the whole mushrooms, unsliced. They seem to keep fresh for longer.

Measurement Conversions

OVEN TEMPERATURES

FAHRENHEIT	CELSIUS (APPROXIMATE)
250°F	120°C
300°F	150°C
325°F	165°C
350°F	180°C
375°F	190°C
400°F	200°C
425°F	220°C
450°F	230°C

VOLUME EQUIVALENTS (LIQUID)

US STANDARD	US STANDARD (OUNCES)	METRIC (APPROXIMATE)
2 tablespoons	1 fl. oz.	30 mL
¼ cup	2 fl. oz.	60 mL
½ cup	4 fl. oz.	120 mL
1 cup	8 fl. oz.	240 mL
1½ cups	12 fl. oz.	355 mL
2 cups or 1 pint	16 fl. oz.	475 mL
4 cups or 1 quart	32 fl. oz.	1 L
1 gallon	128 fl. oz.	4 L

WEIGHT EQUIVALENTS

US STANDARD	METRIC (APPROXIMATE)
½ ounce	15 g
1 ounce	30 g
2 ounces	60 g
4 ounces	115 g
8 ounces	225 g
12 ounces	340 g
16 ounces, or 1 pound	455 g

VOLUME EQUIVALENTS (DRY)

US STANDARD	METRIC (APPROXIMATE)
⅛ teaspoon	0.5 mL
¼ teaspoon	1 mL
½ teaspoon	2 mL
¾ teaspoon	4 mL
1 teaspoon	5 mL
1 tablespoon	15 mL
¼ cup	59 mL
⅓ cup	79 mL
½ cup	118 mL
⅔ cup	156 mL
¾ cup	177 mL
1 cup	235 mL
2 cups or 1 pint	475 mL
3 cups	700 mL
4 cups or 1 quart	1 L

Resources

KingArthurBaking.com
This is an excellent website run by my favorite flour company, King Arthur Flour. This company sells the highest-quality flour, and the website has loads of great information like recipes and troubleshooting tips.

***The Pastry Chef's Little Black Book* by Michael Zebrowski and Michael Mignano**
I've had this book for many years, and it is easily one of my most-referenced cookbooks. Not only does it have great recipes for doughs and fillings, it has everything pastry-related you could think of.

***The Pastry School: Sweet and Savoury Pies, Tarts and Treats to Bake at Home*
by Julie Jones**
This book is fantastic for pie decoration inspiration and has some amazing sweet and savory fillings.

Williams-Sonoma.com
Williams Sonoma is my all-time favorite store for all things kitchen and equipment. It sells high-quality tools and equipment perfect for your home kitchen or a gift for a loved one.

Index

Acknowledgments

To Callisto Media, thank you so much for allowing me to contribute these variations of pie to the world. To my editor, Marjorie, thank you for allowing me to be as creative as I could, and helping create this book.

To the countless taste testers who helped me eat all the pies, thank you for taking the time to provide helpful and honest feedback and taking home all the leftovers.

Thank you to my husband. You've been my rock, my favorite person to do life with, and fellow food lover. Thank you for not judging me when I've destroyed the oven on several occasions throughout the creation of this book. Thank you for tasting pie even when you didn't want to. And thank you for helping clean a mountain of dishes each day.

To my mom and dad, your love and encouragement throughout my entire life is the reason I am who I am today. I am forever grateful to have you both in my life.

To my KTRG family, thank you for helping shape me into the chef I am today.

About the Author

 SAURA KLINE is a professional pastry chef, dessert blogger, and cookbook author. She grew up in Los Angeles, California, and has been cooking in professional kitchens for over a decade. Originally drawn to the beautiful design of wedding cakes, she ultimately found her passion in creating restaurant-quality desserts. Saura now lives in Denver, Colorado, with her husband and their bull terrier. She is currently the executive pastry chef for the Kevin Taylor Restaurant Group, where she creates menus and pastries for three restaurants.

Saura is the author of *Easy as Pie: The Essential Pie Cookbook for Every Season and Reason* and has contributed as a recipe developer for Yummly. She also started a dessert blog in 2017, SweetSaura.com, where she shares her favorite recipes so dessert lovers can easily recreate them at home.

CPSIA information can be obtained
at www.ICGtesting.com
Printed in the USA
JSHW051559271220
10553JS00004B/15

9 781647 399931